Prayers That Avail Much
Commemorative Leather Edition

**Three Bestselling Volumes
Complete in One Book**

James 5:16

by
Germaine Copeland
Word Ministries, Inc.

And this is the confidence that we have in him, that, if we ask any thing according to his will, he heareth us: and if we know that he hear us, whatsoever we ask, we know that we have the petitions that we desired of him.

1 John 5:14,15

Harrison House
Tulsa, Oklahoma

Prayers That Avail Much Commemorative Leather Edition
ISBN 1-57794-121-7
Copyright © 1997 by Germaine Copeland
Word Ministries, Inc.
38 Sloan St.
Roswell, Georgia 30075

Reprinted 1999

Published by Harrison House, Inc.
P. O. Box 35035
Tulsa, Oklahoma 74153

Presented to

Cheryl Barnes
_____

By

_____

Date

_____

Occasion

_____

Contents

A Word to the Reader

Beloved in Christ,

As the *Prayers That Avail Much* family has grown over the years, we have been thankful to God Who has given us the grace to bring His Word to you in a style and format that reaches into your day-to-day life to bring answered prayer. The many testimonies we receive of healing and deliverance continue to remind us of God's unfailing Word and of His great faithfulness to His children.

We pray this special gift edition will help you to receive the answers you need and through these Scriptures you will come to know our wonderful Savior in a greater and more intimate way.

This book in no way should replace the time you spend meditating in God's Word and seeking His direction. Instead, it is designed to enhance your ability to pray effectively for specific needs. Never forget the power of prayer, for it is the very foundation that enables us to go from faith to faith and glory to glory.

Sincerely in His love,

Germaine Copeland
President
Word Ministries, Inc.

Foreword

The prayers in this book are to be used by you for yourself and for others. They are a matter of the heart. Deliberately feed them into your spirit. Allow the Holy Spirit to make the Word a reality in your heart. Your spirit will become quickened to God's Word, and you will begin to think like God thinks and talk like He talks. You will find yourself poring over His Word — hungering for more and more. The Father rewards those who diligently seek Him. (Heb. 11:6.)

Meditate upon the Scriptures listed with these prayers. These are by no means the only Scriptures on certain subjects, but they are a beginning.

These prayers are to be a help and a guide to you in order for you to get better acquainted with your heavenly Father and His Word. Not only does His Word affect your life, but also it will affect others through you, for you will be able to counsel accurately those who come to you for advice. If you cannot counsel someone with the Word, you do not have anything with which to counsel. Walk in God's counsel, and prize His wisdom. (Ps. 1; Prov. 4:7,8.)

People are looking for something on which they can depend. When someone in need comes to you, you can point him to that portion in God's Word that is the answer to his problem. You become victorious, trustworthy, and the one with the answer, for your heart is fixed and established on His Word. (Ps. 112.)

Once you begin delving into God's Word, you must commit to ordering your conversation aright. (Ps. 50:23.) That is being a doer of the Word. Faith always has a good report. You cannot pray effectively for yourself, for someone else, or about something and then talk negatively about the matter. (Matt. 12:34-37.) This is being double-minded, and a double-minded man receives *nothing* from God. (James 1:6-8.)

In Ephesians 4:29-30 AMP it is written:

> Let no foul or polluting language, nor evil
> word, nor unwholesome or worthless talk [ever]
> come out of your mouth; but only such [speech]
> as is good and beneficial to the spiritual progress
> of others, as is fitting to the need and the occa-
> sion, that it may be a blessing and give grace
> (God's favor) to those who hear it.

Praise God for His Word and the limitlessness of prayer in the name of Jesus. It belongs to every child of God. Therefore, run with patience the race that is set before you, looking unto Jesus the author and finisher of your faith. (Heb. 12:1,2.) God's Word is able to build you up and give you your rightful inheritance among all God's set apart ones. (Acts 20:32.)

Commit yourself to pray and to pray correctly by approaching the throne with your mouth filled with His Word!

Introduction

> ...The earnest (heart-felt, continued) prayer
> of a righteous man makes tremendous power
> available — dynamic in its working.
>
> James 5:16 AMP

Prayer is fellowshiping with the Father — a vital, personal contact with God Who is more than enough. We are to be in constant communion with Him:

> For the eyes of the Lord are upon the right-
> eous — those who are upright and in right stand-
> ing with God — and His ears are attentive (open)
> to their prayer....
>
> 1 Peter 3:12 AMP

Prayer is not to be a religious form with no power. It is to be effective and accurate and bring *results*. God watches over His Word to perform it. (Jer. 1:12).

Prayer that brings results must be based on God's Word.

> For the Word that God speaks is alive and
> full of power — making it active, operative,

energizing and effective; it is sharper than any
two-edged sword, penetrating to the dividing
line of the breath of life (soul) and [the immor-
tal] spirit, and of joints and marrow [that is, of
the deepest parts of our nature] exposing and
sifting and analyzing and judging the very
thoughts and purposes of the heart.

Hebrews 4:12 AMP

Prayer is this "living" Word in our mouths. Our
mouths must speak forth faith, for faith is what pleases
God. (Heb. 11:6.) We hold His Word up to Him in
prayer, and our Father sees Himself in His Word.

God's Word is our contact with Him. We put
Him in remembrance of His Word (Isa. 43:26)
placing a demand on His ability in the name of our
Lord Jesus. We remind Him that He supplies all of
our needs according to His riches in glory by Christ
Jesus. (Phil. 4:19.) That Word does not return to Him
void — without producing any effect, useless — but it
shall accomplish that which He pleases and purposes,
and it shall prosper in the thing for which He sent it.
(Isa. 55:11.) Hallelujah!

God did *not* leave us without His thoughts and His ways for we have His Word — His bond. God instructs us to call Him, and He will answer and show us great and mighty things. (Jer. 33:3.) Prayer is to be exciting — not drudgery.

It takes someone to pray. God moves as we pray in faith — believing. He says that His eyes run to and fro throughout the whole earth to show Himself strong in behalf of those whose hearts are blameless toward Him. (2 Chron. 16:9.) We are blameless. (Eph. 1:4.) We are His very own children. (Eph. 1:5.) We are His right-eousness in Christ Jesus. (2 Cor. 5:21.) He tells us to come boldly to the throne of grace and *obtain* mercy and find grace to help in time of need — appropriate and well-timed help. (Heb. 4:16.) Praise the Lord!

The prayer armor is for every believer, every member of the Body of Christ, who will put it on and walk in it, for the weapons of our warfare are *not carnal* but mighty through God for the pulling down of the strongholds of the enemy (Satan, the god of this world, and all his demonic forces). Spiritual warfare takes place in prayer. (2 Cor. 10:4; Eph. 6:12,18.)

There are many different kinds of prayer, such as the prayer of thanksgiving and praise, the prayer of dedication and worship, and the prayer that changes *things* (not God). All prayer involves a time of fellowshiping with the Father.

In Ephesians 6, we are instructed to take the Sword of the Spirit which is the Word of God and **pray at all times — on every occasion, in every season — in the Spirit, with all [manner of] prayer and entreaty** (Eph. 6:18 AMP).

In 1 Timothy 2 we are admonished and urged that **petitions, prayers, intercessions and thanksgivings be offered on behalf of all men** (1 Tim 2:1 AMP). *Prayer is our responsibility.*

Prayer must be the foundation of every Christian endeavor. Any failure is a prayer failure. We are *not* to be ignorant concerning God's Word. God desires for His people to be successful, to be filled with a full, deep, and clear knowledge of His will (His Word), and to bear fruit in every good work. (Col. 1:9-13.) We then bring honor and glory to Him. (John 15:8.) He desires that we know how to pray for **the prayer of the upright is his delight** (Prov. 15:8).

Our Father has not left us helpless. Not only has He given us His Word, but also He has given us the Holy Spirit to help our infirmities when we know not how to pray as we ought. (Rom. 8:26.) Praise God! Our Father has provided His people with every possible avenue to ensure their complete and total victory in this life in the name of our Lord Jesus. (1 John 5:3-5.)

We pray to the Father, in the name of Jesus, through the Holy Spirit, according to the Word!

Using God's Word on purpose, specifically, in prayer is one means of prayer, and it is a most effective and accurate means. Jesus said, **The words (truths) that I have been speaking to you are spirit and life** (John 6:63 AMP).

When Jesus faced Satan in the wilderness, He said, "It is written...it is written...it is written." We are to live, be upheld, and sustained by every Word that proceeds from the mouth of God. (Matt. 4:4.)

James, by the Spirit, admonishes that we do not have, because we do not ask. We ask and receive not, because we ask amiss. (James 4:2,3.) We must heed that admonishment now for we are to become experts in prayer rightly dividing the Word of Truth. (2 Tim. 2:15.)

Using the Word in prayer is *not* taking it out of context, for His Word in us is the key to answered prayer — to prayer that brings results. He is able to do exceedingly abundantly above all we ask or think, according to the power that works in us. (Eph. 3:20.) The power lies within God's Word. It is anointed by the Holy Spirit. The Spirit of God does not lead us apart from the Word, for the Word is of the Spirit of God. We apply that Word personally to ourselves and to others — not adding to or taking from it — in the name of Jesus. We apply the Word to the *now* — to those things, circumstances, and situations facing each of us *now*.

Paul was very specific and definite in his praying. The first chapters of Ephesians, Philippians, Colossians, and 2 Thessalonians are examples of how Paul prayed for believers. There are numerous others. *Search them out.* Paul wrote under the inspiration of the Holy Spirit. We can use these Spirit-given prayers today!

In 2 Corinthians 1:11, 2 Corinthians 9:14, and Philippians 1:4, we see examples of how believers prayed one for another — putting others first in their prayer life with *joy*. Our faith does work by love. (Gal. 5:6.) We grow spiritually as we reach out to help others — praying for and with them and holding out to them the Word of Life. (Phil. 2:16.)

Man is a spirit, he has a soul, and he lives in a body. (1 Thess. 5:23.) In order to operate successfully, each of these three parts must be fed properly. The soul or intellect feeds on intellectual food to produce intellectual strength. The body feeds on physical food to produce physical strength. The spirit — the heart or inward man — is the real you, the part that has been reborn in Christ Jesus. It must feed on spirit food which is God's Word in order to produce and develop faith. As we feast upon God's Word, our minds become renewed with His Word, and we have a fresh mental and spiritual attitude. (Eph. 4:23,24.)

Likewise, we are to present our bodies a living sacrifice, holy, acceptable unto God (Rom. 12:1) and not let that body dominate us but bring it into subjection to the spirit man. (1 Cor. 9:27.) God's Word is healing and health to all our flesh. (Prov. 4:22.) Therefore, God's Word affects each part of us — spirit, soul and body. We become vitally united to the Father, to Jesus, and to the Holy Spirit — one with Them. (John 16:13-15, John 17:21, Col. 2:10.)

God's Word, this spirit food, takes root in our hearts, is formed by the tongue, and is spoken out of our mouths. This is creative power. The spoken Word works as we confess it and then apply the action to it.

Be doers of the Word, and not hearers only, deceiving your own selves. (James 1:22.) Faith without works or corresponding action is *dead*. (James 2:17.) Don't be mental assenters — those who agree that the Bible is true but never act on it. *Real faith is acting on God's Word now.* We cannot build faith without practicing the Word. We cannot develop an effective prayer life that is anything but empty words unless God's Word actually has a part in our lives. We are to hold fast to our *confession* of the Word's truthfulness. Our Lord Jesus is the High Priest of our confession (Heb. 3:1), and He is the Guarantee of a better agreement — a more excellent and advantageous covenant. (Heb. 7:22.)

Prayer does not cause faith to work, but faith causes prayer to work. Therefore, any prayer problem is a problem of doubt — doubting the integrity of the

Word and the ability of God to stand behind His promises or the statements of fact in the Word.

We can spend fruitless hours in prayer if our hearts are not prepared beforehand. Preparation of the heart, the spirit, comes from meditation in the Father's Word, meditation on who we are in Christ, what He is to us, and what the Holy Spirit can mean to us as we become God-inside minded. As God told Joshua (Josh. 1:8), as we meditate on the Word day and night, and do according to all that is written, then shall we make our way prosperous and have good success. We are to attend to God's Word, submit to His sayings, keep them in the center of our hearts, and put away contrary talk. (Prov. 4:20-24.)

When we use God's Word in prayer, this is *not* something we just rush through uttering once, and we are finished. Do *not* be mistaken. There is nothing "magical" nor "manipulative" about it — no set pattern or device in order to satisfy what we want or think out of our flesh. Instead we are holding God's Word before Him. We confess what He says belongs to us.

We expect His divine intervention while we choose not to look at the things that are seen but at the things that

are unseen, for the things that are seen are subject to change.
(2 Cor. 4:18.)

Prayer based upon the Word rises above the senses, contacts the Author of the Word and sets His spiritual laws into motion. It is not just saying prayers that gets results, but it is spending time with the Father, learning His wisdom, drawing on His strength, being filled with His quietness, and basking in His love that bring results to our prayers. Praise the Lord!

* * *

The prayers in this book are designed to teach and train you in the art of personal confession and intercessory prayer. As you pray them, you will be reinforcing the prayer armor which we have been instructed to put on in Ephesians 6:11. The fabric from which the armor is made is the Word of God. We are to live by every word that proceeds from the mouth of God. We desire the whole counsel of God, because we know it changes us. By receiving that counsel, you will be ... **transformed (changed) by the [entire] renewal of your mind — by its new ideals and attitude — so that you may prove [for yourselves] what is the good and acceptable and perfect** will of God, even the thing which is good and acceptable and perfect [in His sight for you] (Rom. 12:2 AMP).

The prayers of personal confession of the Word of God for yourself can also be used as intercessory prayers for others by simply praying them in the third person, changing the pronouns *I* or *we* to the name of the person or persons for whom you are interceding and adjusting the verbs accordingly.

The prayers of intercession have blanks in which you (individually or as a group) are to fill in the spaces with the name of the person(s) for whom you are praying. These prayers of intercession can likewise be made into prayers of personal confession for yourself (or your group) by inserting your own name(s) and the proper personal pronouns in the appropriate places.

An often-asked question is: "How many times should I pray the same prayer?"

The answer is simple: you pray until you know that the answer is fixed in your heart. After that, you need to repeat the prayer whenever adverse circumstances or long delays cause you to be tempted to doubt that your prayer has been heard and your request granted.

The Word of God is your weapon against the temptation to lose heart and grow weary in your prayer life. When that Word of promise becomes fixed in your heart, you will find yourself praising, giving glory to God for the answer, even when the only evidence you have of that answer is your own faith.

Another question often asked is: "When we repeat prayers more than once, aren't we praying 'vain repetitions'?"

Obviously, such people are referring to the admonition of Jesus when He told His disciples: **And when you pray do not (multiply words, repeating the same ones over and over, and) heap up phrases as the Gentiles do, for they think they will be heard for their much speaking** (Matt. 6:7 AMP). Praying the Word of God is not praying the kind of prayer that the "heathen" pray. You will note in 1 Kings 18:25-29 the manner of prayer that was offered to the gods who could not hear. That is not the way you and I pray. The words that we speak are not vain, but they are spirit and life, and mighty through God to the pulling down of strongholds. We have a God Whose eyes are over the righteous and Whose ears are open to us: when we pray, He hears us.

You are the righteousness of God in Christ Jesus, and your prayers will avail much. They will bring salvation to the sinner, deliverance to the oppressed, healing to the sick, and prosperity to the poor. They will usher in the next move of God in the earth. In addition to affecting outward circumstances and other people, your prayers will also have an effect upon you.

In the very process of praying, your life will be changed as you go from faith to faith and from glory to glory.

As a Christian, your first priority is to love the Lord your God with your entire being, and your neighbor as yourself. You are called to be an intercessor, a man or woman of prayer. You are to seek the face of the Lord as you inquire, listen, meditate and consider in the temple of the Lord.

As one of "God's set-apart ones," the will of Lord for your life is the same as it is for the life of every other true believer: **...seek ye first the kingdom of God, and his righteousness; and all these things shall be added unto you** (Matt. 6:33).

Personal Confessions

Jesus is Lord over my spirit, my soul, and my body. (Phil. 2:9-11.)

Jesus has been made unto me wisdom, righteousness, sanctification, and redemption. I can do all things through Christ Who strengthens me. (1 Cor. 1:30, Phil. 4:13.)

The Lord is my shepherd. I do not want. My God supplies all my need according to His riches in glory in Christ Jesus. (Ps. 23, Phil. 4:19.)

I do not fret or have anxiety about anything. I do not have a care. (Phil. 4:6, 1 Pet. 5:6,7.)

I am the Body of Christ. I am redeemed from the curse, because Jesus bore my sicknesses and carried my diseases in His own body. By His stripes I am healed. I forbid any sickness or disease to operate in my body. Every organ, every tissue of my body functions in the perfection in which God created it to function. I honor God and bring glory to Him in my body. (Gal. 3:13, Matt. 8:17, 1 Pet. 2:24, 1 Cor. 6:20.)

I have the mind of Christ and hold the thoughts, feelings, and purposes of His heart. (1 Cor. 2:16.)

I am a believer and not a doubter. I hold fast to my confession of faith. I decide to walk by faith and practice faith. My faith comes by hearing and hearing by the Word of God. Jesus is the author and the developer of my faith. (Heb. 4:14, Heb. 11:6, Rom. 10:17, Heb. 12:2.)

The love of God has been shed abroad in my heart by the Holy Spirit and His love abides in me richly. I keep myself in the Kingdom of light, in love, in the Word, and the wicked one touches me not. (Rom. 5:5, 1 John 4:16, 1 John 5:18.)

I tread upon serpents and scorpions and over all the power of the enemy. I take my shield of faith and quench his every fiery dart. Greater is He Who is in me than he who is in the world. (Ps. 91:13, Eph. 6:16, 1 John 4:4.)

I am delivered from this present evil world. I am seated with Christ in heavenly places. I reside in the Kingdom of God's dear Son. The law of the Spirit of life in Christ Jesus has made me free from the law of sin and death. (Gal. 1:4, Eph. 2:6, Col. 1:13, Rom. 8:2.)

I fear *not* for God has given me a spirit of power, of love, and of a sound mind. God is on my side. (2 Tim. 1:7, Rom. 8:31.)

I hear the voice of the Good Shepherd. I hear my Father's voice, and the voice of a stranger I will not follow. I roll my works upon the Lord. I commit and trust them wholly to Him. He will cause my thoughts to become agreeable to His will, and so shall my plans be established and succeed. (John 10:27, Prov. 16:3.)

I am a world overcomer because I am born of God. I represent the Father and Jesus well. I am a useful member in the Body of Christ. I am His workmanship recreated in Christ Jesus. My Father God is all the while effectually at work in me both to will and do His good pleasure. (1 John 5:4,5, Eph. 2:10, Phil. 2:13.)

I let the Word dwell in me richly. He Who began a good work in me will continue until the day of Christ. (Col. 3:16, Phil. 1:6.)

Personal
Prayers

part
one

To Receive Jesus as Savior and Lord

Father, it is written in Your Word that if I confess with my mouth that Jesus is Lord and believe in my heart that You have raised Him from the dead, I shall be saved. Therefore, Father, I confess that Jesus is my Lord. I make Him Lord of my life right now. I believe in my heart that You raised Jesus from the dead. I renounce my past life with Satan and close the door to any of his devices.

I thank You for forgiving me of all my sin. Jesus is my Lord, and I am a new creation. Old things have passed away. Now all things become new in Jesus' name. Amen.

Scripture References

John 3:16	John 14:6
John 6:37	Romans 10:9,10
John 10:10b	Romans 10:13
Romans 3:23	Ephesians 2:1-10
2 Corinthians 5:19	2 Corinthians 5:17
John 16:8,9	John 1:12
Romans 5:8	2 Corinthians 5:21

To Pray

Father, in the name of Jesus, I offer up thanksgiving that You have called me to be a fellow workman — a joint promoter and a laborer together — with and for You. I commit myself to pray and not to turn coward — faint, lose heart, or give up.

Fearlessly and confidently and boldly I draw near to the throne of grace that I may receive mercy and find grace to help in good time for every need — appropriate help and well-timed help, coming just when I (and others) need it. This is the confidence that I have in You, that, if I ask anything according to Your will, You hear me: and if I know that You hear me, whatsoever I ask, I know that I have the petitions that I desired of You.

When I do not know what prayer to offer and how to offer it worthily as I ought, I thank You, Father, that the (Holy) Spirit comes to my aid and bears me up in my weakness (my inability to produce results). He, the Holy Spirit, goes to meet my supplication and pleads in my behalf with unspeakable yearnings and groanings too deep for utterance. And He Who searches the hearts of men knows what is in the mind of the (Holy) Spirit. The Holy Spirit intercedes and pleads in behalf of the saints according to and in harmony with God's will. Therefore, I am assured and know that (God being a partner in my labor) all things work together and are [fitting into a plan] for my good, because I love God and am called according to [His] design and purpose.

I do not fret or have any anxiety about anything, but in every circumstance and in everything by prayer and petition [definite requests] with thanksgiving continue to make my wants (and the wants of others) known to God. Whatever I ask for in prayer, I believe that it is granted to me, and I will receive it.

The earnest (heartfelt, continued) prayer of a right-eous man makes tremendous power available — dynamic in its working. Father, I live in You — abide vitally united to You — and Your words remain in me and continue to live in my heart. Therefore I ask what-ever I will and it shall be done for me. When I bear (produce) much fruit (through prayer), You, Father, are honored and glorified. Hallelujah! Amen.

Scripture References

1 Corinthians 3:9 AMP   Philippians 4:6 AMP

Luke 18:1 AMP   Mark 11:24 AMP

Hebrews 4:16 AMP   James 5:16b AMP

1 John 5:14,15   John 15:7,8 AMP

Romans 8:26-29 AMP

To Be God-Inside Minded

I am a spirit, I have a soul, and I live in a physical body. My spirit is the candle of the Lord. God, my Father, is guiding me into all the truth through my spirit.

I am a child of God, born of the Spirit of God, filled with the Spirit of God, and led by the Spirit of God. I listen to my heart as I look to my spirit inside me.

The Holy Spirit gives direction to my spirit and illumination to my mind. He leads me in the way I should go in all the affairs of life. He leads me by an inward witness. The eyes of my understanding are being enlightened. Wisdom is in my inward parts. His love is perfected in me. I have an unction from the Holy One.

I am becoming spirit-conscious. I listen to the voice of my spirit and obey what my spirit tells me. I let my spirit dominate me, for I walk not after the flesh, but after the spirit. I examine my leading in the light of His Word. I trust in the Lord with all my heart and lean not to my own understanding. In all my ways I acknowledge Him, and He directs my paths. I walk in the light of God's Word.

I will educate and train and develop my human spirit. The Word of God shall not depart out of my mouth. I meditate therein day and night. Therefore I shall make my way prosperous, and I will have good success in life. *I am a doer of the Word and put God's Word first.* My spirit man is in the ascendancy.

Thanks be unto God who always causes me to triumph in Christ!

In Jesus' name I pray, amen.

Scripture References

1 Thessalonians 5:23	Job 38:36
Proverbs 20:27	1 John 4:12
John 16:13	1 John 2:20
Romans 8:14,16	Romans 9:1
John 3:6,7	Romans 8:1
John 7:37-39	Proverbs 3:5,6
Ephesians 5:18	Psalm 119:105
Isaiah 48:17	Joshua 1:8
Ephesians 1:18	James 1:22

To Put on the Armor of God

In the name of Jesus, I put on the whole armor of God, that I may be able to stand against the wiles of the devil, for I wrestle not against flesh and blood, but against principalities, powers, the rulers of the darkness of this world, and against spiritual wickedness in high places.

Therefore, I take unto myself the whole armor of God, that I may be able to withstand in the evil day, and having done all, to stand. I stand, therefore, having my loins girt about with truth. Your Word, Lord, which is truth, contains all the weapons of my warfare which are not carnal, but mighty through God to the pulling down of strongholds.

I have on the breastplate of righteousness; which is faith and love. My feet are shod with the preparation of the Gospel of peace. In Christ Jesus I have peace, and pursue peace with all men. I am a minister of reconciliation proclaiming the good news of the Gospel.

I take the shield of faith, wherewith I am able to quench all the fiery darts of the wicked, the helmet of salvation *(holding the thoughts, feelings and purpose of God's heart)* and the sword of the Spirit, which is the Word of God. In the face of all trials, tests, temptations and tribulation, I cut to pieces the snare of the enemy by speaking the Word of God. Greater is He that is in me than he that is in the world.

Thank You, Father, for the armor. I will pray at all times — on every occasion, in every season — in the Spirit, with all [manner of] prayer and entreaty. To that end I will keep alert and watch with strong purpose and perseverance, interceding in behalf of all the saints. My power and ability and sufficiency are from God Who has qualified me as a minister and a dispenser of a new covenant [of salvation through Christ]. Amen.

Scripture References

Ephesians 6:11-14a	Psalm 34:14
John 17:17b	2 Corinthians 5:18
2 Corinthians 10:4	Ephesians 6:16, 17 AMP
Ephesians 6:14b,15 AMP	1 John 4:4b
Ephesians 2:14	2 Corinthians 3:5,6 AMP

To Rejoice in the Lord

Father, this is the day the Lord has made. I rejoice and I am glad in it! I rejoice in You always. And again I say, I rejoice. I delight myself in You, Lord. Happy am I because God is my Lord!

Father, You say that You rejoice over me with joy. Hallelujah! I am redeemed. I come with singing, and everlasting joy is upon my head. I obtain joy and gladness, and sorrow and sighing flee away. That spirit of rejoicing, joy, and laughter is my heritage. Where the Spirit of the Lord is there is liberty — emancipation from bondage, freedom. I walk in that liberty.

Father, my mouth shall praise You with joyful lips. I am ever filled and stimulated with the Holy Spirit. I speak out in psalms and hymns and make melody with all my heart to You, Lord. My happy heart is a good medicine and my cheerful mind works healing. The light in my eyes rejoices the heart of others. I have a good report. My countenance radiates the joy of the Lord.

Father, I thank You that I bear much prayer fruit. I ask in Jesus' name, and I will receive so that my joy (gladness, delight) may be full, complete, and overflowing. That joy of the Lord is my *strength*. Therefore, I can count it all joy, all strength, when I encounter tests or trials of any sort because I am strong in You, Father.

I have the *victory* in the name of Jesus. Satan is under my feet. I am not moved by adverse circumstances. I have been made the righteousness of God in Christ Jesus. I dwell in the Kingdom of God and have peace and joy in the Holy Spirit! Praise the Lord!

In Jesus' name I pray, amen.

Scripture References

Psalm 118:24	Philippians 4:8
Philippians 4:4	Proverbs 15:13
Philippians 3:1	John 15:7,8
Psalm 144:15	John 16:23
Zephaniah 3:17	Nehemiah 8:10
Isaiah 51:11	James 1:2

2 Corinthians 3:17   Ephesians 6:10
James 1:25   1 John 5:4
Psalm 63:5   Ephesians 1:22
Ephesians 5:18,19   2 Corinthians 5:7
Proverbs 17:22   2 Corinthians 5:21
Proverbs 15:30   Romans 14:17

To Glorify God

In view of [all] the mercies of God, I make a decisive dedication of my body — presenting all my members and faculties — as a living sacrifice, holy (devoted, consecrated) and well pleasing to You, God, which is my reasonable (rational, intelligent) service and spiritual worship. It is [not in my own strength] for it is You, Lord, Who is all the while effectually at work in me — energizing and creating in me the power and desire — both to will and work for Your good pleasure and satisfaction and delight.

Father, I will not draw back or shrink in fear, for then Your soul would have no delight or pleasure in me. I was bought for a price — purchased with a preciousness and paid for, made Your very own. So, then, I honor You, Lord, and bring glory to You in my body.

I called on You in the day of trouble; You delivered me, and I shall honor and glorify you. I rejoice because You delivered me and drew me to Yourself out of the control and dominion of darkness *(obscurity)* and transferred me into the kingdom of the Son of Your love. I will confess and praise You, O Lord my God, with my whole (united) heart; and I will glorify Your name for evermore.

As a bond servant of Jesus Christ, I receive and develop the talents which have been given me, for I would have You say of me, "Well done, you upright (honorable, admirable) and faithful servant!" I make use of the gifts (faculties, talents, qualities) according to the grace given me. I let my light so shine before men that they may see my moral excellence and my praiseworthy, noble and good deeds, and recognize and honor and praise and glorify my Father Who is in heaven.

In the name of Jesus, I allow my life to lovingly express truth in all things — speaking truly, dealing truly, living truly. Whatever I do — no matter what it is — in word or deed, I do everything in the name of the Lord Jesus and in [dependence upon] His Person, giving praise to God the Father through Him. Whatever may be my task, I work at it heartily (from the soul), as [something done] for the Lord and not for men. To God the Father be all glory and honor and praise. Amen.

Scripture References (AMP)

Romans 12:1	Matthew 25:21
Philippians 2:13	Romans 12:6
Hebrews 10:38b	Matthew 5:16
1 Corinthians 6:20	Ephesians 4:15
Psalm 50:15	Colossians 3:17
Colossians 1:13	Colossians 3:23
Psalm 86:12	

To Walk in God's Wisdom and His Perfect Will

Father, I thank you that the communication of my faith becomes effectual by acknowledging every good thing which is in me in Christ Jesus. I hear the voice of the Good Shepherd. I hear my Father's voice, and the voice of a stranger I will not follow.

Father, I believe in my heart and say with my mouth that *this day the will of God is done in my life*. I walk in a manner worthy of You Lord, fully pleasing to You and desiring to please You in all things, bearing fruit in every good work. Jesus has been made unto me wisdom. I single-mindedly walk in that wisdom expecting to know what to do in every situation and to be on *top* of every circumstance!

I roll my works upon You, Lord, and You make my thoughts agreeable to Your will, and so my plans are established and succeed. You direct my steps and make them sure. I understand and firmly grasp what the will of the Lord is for I am not vague, thoughtless, or foolish. I stand firm and mature in spiritual growth, convinced and fully assured in everything willed by God.

Father, You have destined and appointed me to come progressively to know Your will — that is to perceive, to recognize more strongly and clearly, and to become better and more intimately acquainted with Your will. I thank you, Father, for the Holy Spirit who abides permanently in me and Who guides me into all the Truth — the whole, full Truth — and speaks whatever He hears from the Father and announces and declares to me the things that are to come. I have the mind of Christ and hold the thoughts, feelings, and purposes of His heart.

So, Father, I have entered into that blessed rest by adhering, trusting, and relying on You in the name of Jesus. Hallelujah! Amen.

Scripture References

Philemon 6	Ephesians 5:17 AMP
John 10:27	Colossians 4:12 AMP

John 10:5	Acts 22:14
Colossians 1:9,10 AMP	1 John 2:20,27
1 Corinthians 1:30	1 Corinthians 2:16 AMP
James 1:5-8	Hebrews 4:10
Proverbs 16:3,9 AMP	John 16:13 AMP

To Walk in the Word

Father, in the name of Jesus, *I commit myself to walk in the Word.* Your Word living in me produces Your life in this world. I recognize that Your Word is integrity itself — steadfast, sure, eternal — and I trust my life to its provisions.

You have sent your Word forth into my heart. I let it dwell in me richly in all wisdom. I meditate in it day and night so that I may diligently act on it. The Incorruptible Seed, the Living Word, the Word of Truth, is abiding in my spirit. That Seed is growing mightily in me now, producing Your nature, Your life. It is my counsel, my shield, my buckler, my powerful weapon in battle. The Word is a lamp to my feet and a light to my path. It makes my way plain before me. I do not stumble, for my steps are ordered in the Word.

The Holy Spirit leads and guides me into all the truth. He gives me understanding, discernment, and comprehension so that I am preserved from the snares of the evil one.

I delight myself in You and Your Word. Because of that, You put Your desires within my heart. I commit my way unto You, and You bring it to pass. I am confident that You are at work in me now both to will and to do all Your good pleasure.

I exalt Your Word, hold it in high esteem, and give it first place. *I make my schedule around Your Word.* I make the Word final authority to settle all questions that confront me. I choose to agree with the Word of God, and I choose to disagree with any thoughts, conditions, or circumstances contrary to Your Word. I boldly and confidently say that my heart is fixed and established on the solid foundation — the living Word of God! Amen.

Scripture References

Hebrews 4:12	1 Peter 3:12
Colossians 3:16	Colossians 4:2
Joshua 1:8	Ephesians 6:10
1 Peter 1:23	Luke 18:1
Psalm 91:4	James 5:16
Psalm 119:105	Psalm 37:4,5

Psalm 37:23	Philippians 2:13
Colossians 1:9	2 Corinthians 10:5
John 16:13	Psalm 112:7,8

To Walk in Love

Father, in Jesus' name, I thank You that the love of God has been poured forth into my heart by the Holy Spirit Who has been given to me. I keep and treasure Your Word. The love of and for You, Father, has been perfected and completed in me, and perfect love casts out all fear.

Father, I am Your child, and *I commit to walk in the God kind of love.* I endure long, am patient, and kind. I am never envious and never boil over with jealousy. I am not boastful or vainglorious, and I do not display myself haughtily. I am not rude and unmannerly and I do not act unbecomingly. I do not insist on my own rights or my own way for I am not self-seeking, touchy, fretful or resentful. I take no account of an evil done to me and pay no attention to a suffered wrong. I do not rejoice at injustice and unrighteousness, but I rejoice when right and truth prevail. I bear up under anything and everything that comes. I am ever ready to believe the *best* of others. My hopes are fadeless under all circumstances. I endure everything without weakening because my love never fails.

Father, I *bless* and *pray* for those who persecute me — who are cruel in their attitude toward me. I bless them and do not curse them. Therefore, my love abounds yet more and more in knowledge and in all judgment. I approve things that are excellent. I am sincere and *without offense* till the day of Christ. I am filled with the fruits of righteousness.

Everywhere I go I commit to plant seeds of love. I thank You, Father, for preparing hearts ahead of time to receive this love. I know that these seeds will produce Your love in the hearts to whom they are given.

Father, I thank You that as I flow in Your love and wisdom, people are being blessed by my life and ministry. Father, You make me to find favor, compassion, and loving kindness with others *(name them)*.

I am rooted deep in love and founded securely on love knowing that You are on my side, and nothing is able to separate me from Your love, Father, which is in

Christ Jesus my Lord. Thank You, Father, in Jesus' precious name. Amen.

Scripture References

Romans 5:5	Philippians 1:9-11
1 John 2:5	John 13:34
1 John 4:18	1 Corinthians 3:6
1 Corinthians 13:4-8 AMP	Daniel 1:9 AMP
Romans 12:14 AMP	Ephesians 3:17 AMP
Matthew 5:44	Romans 8:31,39

vessel unto honor, sanctified, and fitting for the Master's use and prepared for every good work.

Thank You, Lord, that I eat the good of the land, because I am willing and obedient. Amen.

Scripture References

Isaiah 1:16,17	2 Corinthians 7:1
1 Corinthians 1:30	2 Timothy 2:21
Ephesians 5:26	1 John 1:8,9
John 17:17	Isaiah 1:19

To Bear Fruit

Lord Jesus, You said in John 15:16 that You have chosen us and ordained us that we should go and bring forth fruit and that our fruit should remain, that whatsoever we shall ask of the Father in Your name, He may give it to us.

The Apostle Paul said to be filled with the fruit of righteousness and that he desired that fruit might abound to our account. Therefore, I commit myself to bring forth the fruit of the spirit: love, joy, peace, long-suffering, gentleness, goodness, faith, meekness, and temperance. I renounce and turn from the fruit of the flesh, because I am Christ's and have crucified the flesh with its affections and lusts.

A seed cannot bear fruit unless it first falls into the ground and dies. I confess that I am crucified with Christ: nevertheless I live; yet not I but Christ lives in me. And the life that I now live in the flesh I live by the faith of the Son of God, Who loved me and gave Himself for me.

Father, I thank You that I am good ground, that I hear Your Word and understand it, and that the Word bears fruit in my life — sometimes a hundredfold, sometimes sixty, sometimes thirty. I am like a tree planted by the rivers of water that brings forth fruit in its season. My leaf shall not wither, and whatever I do shall prosper.

Father, in Jesus' name, I thank You for filling me with the knowledge of Your will in all wisdom and spiritual understanding that I may walk worthy of You, Lord, being fruitful in every good work and increasing in the knowledge of You. Amen.

Scripture References

John 15:16	Galatians 2:20
Philippians 1:11	Matthew 13:23
Philippians 4:17	Psalm 1:3
Galatians 5:22-24	Colossians 1:9,10
John 12:24	

To Help Others

Father, in the name of Jesus, I will do unto others as I would have them do unto me. I eagerly pursue and seek to acquire [this] *(agape)* love — I make it my aim, my great quest in life.

Father, in the name of Jesus, I will esteem and look upon and be concerned for not [merely] my own interest, but also for the interest of others as they pursue success. I am strong in the Lord, and in the power of His might. I will, on purpose, in the name of Jesus, make it a practice to please (make happy) my neighbor, *(boss, co-worker, teacher, parent, child, brother, etc.)* for his good and for his true welfare, to edify him — that is, to strengthen him and build him up in all ways — spiritually, socially and materially.

Father, in the name of Jesus, I will therefore encourage (admonish, exhort) others and edify — strengthen and build up — others.

Father, in the name of Jesus, I love my enemies *(as well as my business associates, fellow church members, neighbors, those in authority over me)* and am kind and do good

— doing favors so that someone derives benefit from them. I lend expecting and hoping for nothing in return, but considering nothing as lost and despairing of no one. Then my recompense (my reward) will be great — rich, strong, intense, and abundant — and I will be a son of the Most High; for He is kind and charitable and good to the ungrateful and selfish and wicked. I am merciful — sympathetic tender, responsive, and compassionate — even as my Father is [all these]. I am an imitator of God, my Father — therefore, I walk in love.

Thank You, Father, for imprinting Your laws upon my heart, and inscribing them on my mind — on my inmost thoughts and understanding. According to Your Word, as I would like and desire that men would do to me, I do exactly so to them, in the name of Jesus. Amen.

Scripture References

Luke 6:31	1 Thessalonians 5:11 AMP
1 Corinthians 14:1 AMP	Luke 6:35,36 AMP
Philippians 2:4 AMP	Ephesians 5:1,2 AMP
Ephesians 6:10	Hebrews 10:16b AMP
Romans 15:2 AMP	Luke 6:31 AMP

To Watch What You Say

Father, today, I make a commitment to You in the name of Jesus. I turn from idle words and foolishly talking things that are contrary to my true desire to myself and toward others. Your Word says that the tongue defiles; that the tongued sets on fire the course of nature; that the tongue is set on fire of hell.

In the name of Jesus, I am determined to take control of my tongue. I am determined that hell will not set my tongue on fire. I renounce, reject, and repent of every word that has ever proceeded out of my mouth against You, God, and Your operation. I cancel its power and dedicate my mouth to speak excellent and right things. My mouth shall utter truth.

I am the righteousness of God. I set the course of my life for obedience, for abundance, for wisdom, for health, and for joy. Everything I speak is becoming to God. I refuse to compromise or err from pure and sound words. The words of my mouth and my deeds shall show forth Your righteousness and Your salvation all of my days. I guard my mouth and my heart with all diligence. I refuse to give Satan any place in me.

Father, Your Words are top priority to me. They are spirit and life. I let the Word dwell in me richly in all wisdom. The ability of God is released within me by the words of my mouth and by the Word of God. I speak Your Words out of my mouth. They are alive in me. You are alive and working in me. So, I can boldly say that my words are words of faith, words of power, words of love, and words of life. They produce good things in my life and in the lives of others. Because I choose Your Words for my lips, I choose Your will for my life, and I go forth in the power of those words to perform them in Jesus' name. Amen.

Scripture References

Ephesians 5:4	Proverbs 21:23
2 Timothy 2:16	Ephesians 4:27
James 3:6	James 1:6
Proverbs 8:6,7	John 6:63
2 Corinthians 5:2	Colossians 3:16
Proverbs 4:23	Philemon 6

To Live Free From Worry

Father, I thank You that I have been delivered from
the power of darkness and translated into the Kingdom
of Your dear Son. *I commit to live free from worry in the
name of Jesus*, for the law of the Spirit of life in Christ
Jesus has made me *free* from the law of sin and death.

I humble myself under Your mighty hand that in
due time You may exalt me. I cast the whole of my cares
(name them) — all my anxieties, all my worries, all my
concerns, once and for all — on You. You care for me
affectionately and care about me watchfully. You sustain
me. You will never allow the consistently righteous to be
moved — made to slip, fall, or fail!

Father, I delight myself in You, and You perfect that
which concerns me.

I cast down imaginations (reasonings) and every
high thing that exalts itself against the knowledge of
You, and bring into captivity every thought to the
obedience of Christ. I lay aside every weight and the sin
of worry which does try so easily to beset me. I run with

patience the race that is set before me, looking unto Jesus, the author and finisher of my faith.

I thank You, Father, that You are able to keep that which I have committed unto You. I think on (fix my mind on) those things that are true, honest, just, pure, lovely, of good report, virtuous, and deserving of praise. I let not my heart be troubled. I abide in Your Words, and Your Words abide in me. Therefore, Father, I do *not* forget what manner of person I am. I look into the perfect law of liberty and continue therein, being *not* a forgetful hearer, but a *doer of the Word* and thus blessed in my doing!

Thank You, Father. *I am carefree.* I walk in that peace which passes all understanding in Jesus' name! Amen.

Scripture References

Colossians 1:13	Hebrews 12:1,2
Romans 8:2	2 Timothy 1:12
1 Peter 5:6,7 AMP	Philippians 4:8
Psalm 55:22	John 14:1
Psalm 138:8	James 1:22-25
2 Corinthians 10:5	Philippians 4:6

Adoration: "Hallowed Be Thy Name"

Our Father, which art in heaven, hallowed be Thy Name.

Bless the Lord, O my soul: and all that is within me, bless Your Holy Name. I adore You and make known to You my adoration and love this day.

I bless Your Name, *Elohim*, the Creator of heaven and earth, Who was in the beginning. It is You Who made me, and You have crowned me with glory and honor. You are the God of might and strength. Hallowed be Thy Name!

I bless Your Name, *El-Shaddai*, the God Almighty of Blessings. You are the Breasty One Who nourishes and supplies. You are All-Bountiful and All-Sufficient. Hallowed be Thy Name!

I bless Your Name, *Adonai*, my Lord and my Master. You are Jehovah — the Completely Self-Existing One, always present, revealed in Jesus Who is the same yesterday, today and forever. Hallowed be Thy Name!

I bless Your Name, *Jehovah-Jireh*, the One Who sees my needs and provides for them. Hallowed be Thy Name!

I bless Your Name, *Jehovah-Rapha*, my Healer and the One Who makes bitter experiences sweet. You sent Your Word and healed me. You forgave all my iniquities and You healed all my diseases. Hallowed be Thy Name!

I bless Your Name, *Jehovah-M'Kaddesh*, the Lord my Sanctifier. You have set me apart for Yourself. Hallowed be Thy Name!

Jehovah-Nissi, You are my Victory, my Banner, and my Standard. Your banner over me is love. When the enemy shall come in like a flood, You will lift up a standard against him. Hallowed be Thy Name!

Jehovah-Shalom, I bless Your Name. You are my Peace — the peace which transcends all understanding, which garrisons and mounts guard over my heart and mind in Christ Jesus. Hallowed be Thy Name!

I bless You, *Jehovah-Tsidkenu*, my Righteousness. Thank You for becoming sin for me that I might become the righteousness of God in Christ Jesus. Hallowed be Thy Name!

Jehovah-Rohi, You are my Shepherd and I shall not want for any good or beneficial thing. Hallowed be Thy Name!

Hallelujah to *Jehovah-Shammah* Who will never leave or forsake me. You are always there. I take comfort and am encouraged and confidently and boldly say, The Lord is my Helper, I will not be seized with alarm — I will not fear or dread or be terrified. What can man do to me? Hallowed be Thy Name!

I worship and adore You, *El-Elyon*, the Most High God Who is the First Cause of everything, the Possessor of the heavens and earth. You are the Everlasting-God, the Great-God, the Living-God, the Merciful-God, the Faithful-God, the Mighty-God. You are Truth, Justice, Righteousness, and Perfection. You are *El-Elyon* — the Highest Sovereign of the heavens and the earth. Hallowed be Thy Name!

Father, You have exalted above all else Your Name and Your Word, and You have magnified Your Word above all Your Name! The Word was made flesh, and dwelt among us, and His Name is Jesus! Hallowed be Thy Name!

In Jesus' name I pray, amen.

Scripture References

Matthew 6:9	Song of Solomon 2:4
Psalm 103:1	Isaiah 59:19
Genesis 1:1,2	Judges 6:24
Psalm 8:5b	Philippians 4:7 AMP
Genesis 49:24,25	Jeremiah 23:5,6
Genesis 15:1,2,8	2 Corinthians 5:21
Hebrews 13:8	Psalm 23:1
Genesis 22:14	Psalm 34:10
Psalm 147:3 AMP	Ezekial 48:35
Exodus 15:23-26 AMP	Hebrews 13:5
Psalm 107:20	Hebrews 13:6 AMP
Psalm 103:3	Psalm 91:1
Leviticus 20:7,8	Psalm 138:2 AMP
Exodus 17:15	John 1:14

Divine Intervention: "Thy Kingdom Come"

Father, in Jesus' name, I pray according to Matthew 6:10, Thy Kingdom come. I am looking for the soon coming of our Lord and Savior Jesus Christ.

Today, we are [even here and] now Your children; it is not yet disclosed (made clear) what we shall be [hereafter], *but we know that when He comes and is manifested we shall [as God's children] resemble and be like Him, for we shall see Him just as He [really] is.* You said that everyone who has this hope [resting] on Him cleanses (purifies) himself just as He is pure — chaste, undefiled, guiltless.

For the grace of God — His unmerited favor and blessing — has come forward (appeared) for the deliverance from sin and the eternal salvation for all mankind. It has trained us to reject and renounce all ungodliness (irreligion) and worldly (passionate) desires, to live discreet (temperate, self-controlled), upright, devout (spiritually whole) lives in this present world, awaiting and looking for the [fulfillment, the realization of our] blessed hope, *even the glorious appearing of our great God and Savior Christ Jesus, the Messiah, the Anointed One.*

For the Lord Himself shall descend from heaven with a shout, with the voice of the archangel, and with the trump of God: and the dead in Christ shall rise first. Then we which are alive and remain shall be caught up together with them in the clouds, to meet the Lord in the air: and so shall we ever be with the Lord.

I thank You, Father, that the Lord shall come (to earth), and all the holy ones [saints and angels] with Him; and the Lord shall be King over all the earth; in that day He shall be one Lord, and His name one. The government shall be upon His shoulder.

Father, I thank You that we shall join the great voices in heaven saying, The kingdoms of this world are become the kingdoms of our Lord, and of His Christ; and He shall reign for ever and ever.

Yours, O Lord, is the greatness, and power, and the glory, and the victory, and the majesty; for all that is in the heavens and the earth is Yours; Yours is the

Kingdom, O Lord, and Yours it is to be exalted as head over all. Thy Kingdom come. Hallelujah! Amen.

Scripture References

1 John 3:2,3 AMP   Isaiah 9:6 AMP

Titus 2:11-13 AMP   Revelation 11:15

1 Thessalonians 4:16,17 1 Chronicles 29:11 AMP

Zechariah 14:5,9 AMP

Forgiveness: "Forgive Us Our Debts"

Father, I forgive everyone who has trespassed against me so that You can forgive me my trespasses. [Now, having received the Holy Spirit and being led and directed by Him] if I forgive the sins of anyone they are forgiven; if I retain the sins of anyone, they are retained.

Father, Your Word says, **Love your enemies and pray for those who persecute you** (Matt. 5:44 AMP).

I come before you in Jesus' name to lift _____ before You. I invoke blessings upon him/her and pray for his/her happiness. I implore Your blessings (favor) upon him/her.

Father, not only will I pray for _____, but I set myself to treat him/her well (do good to, act nobly toward him/her). I will be merciful, sympathetic, tender, responsive, and compassionate toward _____ even as You are, Father.

I am an imitator of You, and I can do all things through Christ Jesus Who strengthens me.

Father, I thank You that I have great peace in this situation, for I love Your law and refuse to take offense toward _____.

Jesus, I am blessed — happy [with life — joy and satisfaction in God's favor and salvation apart from outward conditions] and to be envied — because I take no offense in You and refuse to be hurt or resentful or annoyed or repelled or made to stumble, [whatever may occur].

And now, Father, I roll this work upon You — commit and trust it wholly to You; and believe that You will cause my thoughts to become in agreement to Your will, and so my plans shall be established and succeed.

In Jesus' name, amen.

Scripture References

Matthew 6:12   Ephesians 5:1 AMP
Matthew 6:14,15   Philippians 4:13 AMP

John 20:23 AMP   Psalm 119:165 AMP
Luke 6:27b AMP   Luke 7:23 AMP
Matthew 5:44 AMP   Proverbs 16:3 AMP
Luke 6:28 AMP

Guidance and Deliverance: "Lead Us Not Into Temptation"

There has no temptation taken me but such as is common to man: but *God is faithful*, Who will not suffer me to be tempted above that which I am able; but will with the temptation also make a way to escape, that I may be able to bear it.

I count it all joy when I fall into various temptations; knowing this, that the trying of my faith works patience.

I will not say when I am tempted, I am tempted from God; for God is incapable of being tempted by [what is] evil and He Himself tempts no one.

Thank You, Jesus, for giving Yourself for my sins, that You might deliver me from this present evil world, according to the will of God and our Father: to Whom be glory for ever and ever.

Father, in the name of Jesus, and according to the power that is at work in me, I will keep awake (give strict attention, be cautious) and watch and pray that I may not come into temptation. In Jesus' name, amen.

Scripture References

1 Corinthians 10:13	Galatians 1:4,5
James 1:2,3	Ephesians 3:20b
James 1:13 AMP	Matthew 26:41a AMP

Praise: "For Thine Is the Kingdom, and the Power, and the Glory"

O magnify the Lord with me, and let us exalt His name together.

As for God, His way is perfect! The Word of the Lord is tested and tried; He is a shield to all those who take refuge and put their trust in Him.

Let the words of my mouth and the meditation of my heart be acceptable in Your sight, O Lord, my firm, impenetrable rock and my redeemer.

Your Word has revived me and given me life.

Forever, O Lord, Your Word is settled in heaven.

Your Word is a lamp to my feet and a light to my path.

The sum of Your Word is truth and every one of Your righteous decrees endures forever.

I will worship toward Your holy temple, and praise Your name for Your loving-kindness and for Your truth and faithfulness; for You have exalted above all else Your name and Your Word, and You have magnified Your Word above all Your name!

Let my prayer be set forth as incense before You, the lifting up of my hands as the evening sacrifice. Set a guard, O Lord, before my mouth; keep watch at the door of my lips.

He who brings an offering of praise and thanksgiving honors and glorifies Me; and he who orders his way aright — who prepares the way that I may show him — to him I will demonstrate the salvation of God.

My mouth shall be filled with Your praise and with Your honor all the day.

Because Your loving-kindness is better than life, my lips shall praise You. So will I bless You while I live; I will lift up my hands in Your name.

Your testimonies also are my delight and my counselors.

In Jesus' name I pray, amen.

Scripture References

Psalm 34:3	Psalm 138:2
Psalm 18:30	Psalm 141:2,3
Psalm 19:14	Psalm 50:23
Psalm 119:50	Psalm 71:8
Psalm 119:89	Psalm 63:3,4
Psalm 119:105	Psalm 119:24
Psalm 119:160	

Submitting All to God

Father, You are the Supreme Authority — a God of order. You have instituted other authority structures that will support healthy relationships and maintain harmony. It is my decision to surrender my will to You that I might find protection and dwell in the secret place of the Most High.

Father, thank You for pastors and leaders of the church — those who are submitted to You and are examples to the congregation. I submit to the church elders (the ministers and spiritual guides of the church) — [giving them due respect and yielding to their counsel].

Lord, You know just how rebellious I have been. I ask Your forgiveness for manipulating circumstances and people — for trying to manipulate You to get my own way. May Your will be done in my life, even as it is in heaven.

Father, my life is out of control, and I submit myself to You. I resist the devil, and he will flee from me.

Obedience is far better than sacrifice. Father, You are much more interested in my listening to You than in my offerings of material things to You. Rebellion is as bad as the sin of witchcraft, and stubbornness is as bad as worshiping idols. Forgive me for practicing witchcraft and worshiping idols.

Father, You deserve honesty from the heart; yes, utter sincerity and truthfulness. Oh, give me this wisdom. Sprinkle me with the cleansing blood and I shall be clean again. Wash me and I shall be whiter than snow. You have rescued me from the dominion of darkness and brought me into the Kingdom of the Son You love, in Whom I have redemption, the forgiveness of sins.

Lord, I want to follow You. I am putting aside my own desires and conveniences. I yield my desires that are not in Your plan for me. Even in the midst of my fear I surrender and entrust my future to You. I choose to take up my cross and follow You [cleave steadfastly to You, conforming wholly to Your example in living and, if need be, in dying also]. I desire to lose my [lower life] on Your account that I might find it [the higher life].

Father, You gave Jesus to be my Example. He has returned to You, Father, and has sent the Holy Spirit to be my Helper and Guide. In this world there are temptations, trials, and tribulations, but Jesus has overcome the world, and I am of good cheer.

Jesus is my Lord. I choose to become His servant. He calls me His friend.

Lord, help me to walk through the process of surrendering my all to You. I exchange rebellion and stubbornness for a willing and obedient heart — when I refuse to listen, anoint my ears to hear; when I am blinded by my own desires, open my eyes to see.

I belong to Jesus Christ, the Anointed One Who breaks down and destroys every yoke of bondage. In His name and in obedience to Your will, Father, I submit to the control and direction of the Holy Spirit Whom You have sent to live in me. I am Your child. All to You I surrender. I am an overcomer by the blood of the Lamb, and by the word of my testimony!

In Jesus' name I pray, amen.

Scripture References

1 Corinthians 14:33	Psalm 51:6,7 TLB
1 Timothy 2:2	Colossians 1:13,14 NIV
Psalm 91:1	Matthew 10:38,39 AMP
1 Peter 5:5 AMP	John 16:33
Matthew 6:10	John 15:15
James 4:7	Revelation 12:11
1 Samuel 15:22,23 TLB	

Receiving Forgiveness

Father, Your Word declares that if I ask for forgiveness, You will forgive me and cleanse me from all unrighteousness. Help me to believe; help me to receive my forgiveness for past and present sins. Help me to forgive myself. I confess Jesus as my Lord and believe in my heart that You raised Him from the dead, and I am saved.

Father, Your Son Jesus said that whatever I ask for in prayer, having faith and really believing, I will receive. Lord, I believe, help my unbelief.

Father, I count myself blessed, how happy I am — I get a fresh start, my slate's wiped clean. I count myself blessed (happy, fortunate, to be envied) — You, Father, are holding nothing against me and You're not holding anything back from me.

When I keep it all inside, my bones turn to powder, my words become daylong groans. The pressure never lets up; all the juices of my life dry up. I am letting it all out; I am saying once and for all that I am making a clean breast of my failures to You, Lord.

In the face of this feeling of guilt and unworthiness, I receive my forgiveness and the pressure is gone — my guilt dissolved, my sin disappeared. I am blessed, for You have forgiven my transgressions — You have covered my sins. I am blessed, for You will never count my sins against me.

Father, You chose me [actually picked me out for Yourself as Your very own] in Christ before the foundation of the world, that I should be holy (consecrated and set apart for You) blameless in Your sight, even above reproach, before You in love. In Jesus I have redemption (deliverance and salvation) through His blood, the remission (forgiveness) of my offenses (shortcomings and trespasses), in accordance with the riches and the generosity of Your gracious favor.

Lord, I have received Your Son Jesus, I believe in His name, and He has given me the right to become Your child. I acknowledge You, Lord, as my Father. Thank You for forgiving me and absolving me of all guilt. I am an overcomer by the blood of the Lamb, and by the word of my testimony.

In the name of Jesus, amen.

Scripture References

1 John 1:9	Psalm 32:1-6 MESSAGE
Romans 10:9,10	Romans 4:7,8 NIV
Mark 11:23	Ephesians 1:4,7 AMP
Matthew 21:22 AMP	John 1:12 NIV
Mark 9:24	Revelation 12:11
Psalm 32:1 AMP	

Walking in Humility

Father, I clothe myself with humility [as the garb of a servant, so that its covering cannot possibly be stripped from me]. I renounce pride and arrogance. Father, You give grace to the humble. Therefore I humble myself under Your mighty hand, that in due time You may exalt me.

In the name of Jesus, I cast the whole of my care [all my anxieties, all my worries, all my concerns for my future, once and for all] on You, for You care for me affectionately and care about me watchfully. I expect a life of victory and awesome deeds because my actions are done on behalf of a spirit humbly submitted to Your truth and righteousness.

Father, in the name of Jesus, I refuse to be wise in my own eyes; but I choose to fear You and shun evil. This will bring health to my body and nourishment to my bones.

Father, I humble myself and submit to Your Word that speaks...exposes, sifts, analyzes, and judges the very thoughts and purposes of my heart. I test my own actions, so that I might have appropriate self-esteem, without comparing myself to anyone else. The security of Your guidance will allow me to carry my own load with energy and confidence.

I listen carefully and hear what is being said to me. I incline my ear to wisdom and apply my heart to understanding and insight. Humility and fear of You bring wealth and honor and life.

Father, I hide Your Word in my heart that I might not sin against You. As one of Your chosen people, holy and dearly loved, I clothe myself with compassion, kindness, humility, gentleness, and patience. I bear with others and forgive whatever grievances I may have against anyone. I forgive as You forgave me. And over all these virtues I put on love, which binds them all together in perfect unity. I let the peace of Christ rule in my heart, and I am thankful for Your grace and the power of the Holy Spirit.

Father, may Your will be done on earth in my life as it is in heaven.

In Jesus' name, amen.

Scripture References

1 Peter 5:5-7 AMP

Proverbs 3:7,8 NIV

Hebrews 4:12 AMP

Galatians 6:4,5 NIV

Proverbs 2:2 NIV

Proverbs 22:4 NIV

Psalm 119:11

Colossians 3:12-15 NIV

Matthew 6:10 NIV

Giving Thanks to God

Introduction

God saw you when you were in your mother's womb. (Ps. 139:13-16.) He knew your mother and father and the circumstances of the home where you were to grow up. He knew the schools you would attend and the neighborhood in which you would live.

God gave you the ability to survive and walked with you through good times and bad. He gave you survival techniques and guardian angels to keep and protect you. (Ps. 91:11.) He chose you before the foundation of the world to be holy and without blame before Him in love. (Eph. 1:4.)

He cried with you when you cried. He laughed with you when you laughed. He was grieved when you were misunderstood and treated unfairly. He watched and waited, looking forward to the day when you would receive Jesus as your Savior. To as many as received Him gave He the power, the right, and the authority to become the sons of God. (John 1:12 AMP.) He longs for your fellowship, desiring for you to know Him more and more intimately.

Your survival techniques were probably different from mine. Whatever they were, and whatever your life may have been like up to this point, the peace of God can change the regrets and the wounds of the past into thanksgiving and praise. You can experience wholeness by earnestly and sincerely praying this prayer.

I.

Daily Prayer of Thanksgiving

Father, I come to You in the name of Jesus. With the help of the Holy Spirit, and by Your grace, I join with the heavenly host making a joyful noise to You, and serving You with gladness! I come before Your presence with singing!

Lord, I know (perceive, recognize, and understand with approval) that You are God! It is You Who made us, not we ourselves [and we are Yours]! We are Your people and the sheep of Your pasture.

Father, I enter into Your gates with thanksgiving and present an offering of thanks. I enter into Your courts with praise! I am thankful and delight to say so. I bless and affectionately praise Your name! For You are good and Your mercy and loving-kindness are everlasting. Your faithfulness and truth endure to all generations. It is a good and delightful thing to give thanks to You, O Most High.

Lord, by Your Holy Spirit perfect the fruit of my lips. Help me draw thanksgiving forth from my innermost resources; reach down into the most secret places of my heart that I may offer significant thanksgiving to You, Father.

Thank You for my parents who gave me life. I am grateful for the victories and achievements which I have experienced in spite of my hurts — the bruises and the abuses that boxed me in when I was a small child. You used them for good even though Satan intended them for my destruction.

You prepared me to listen to the inner voice — the voice of Your Holy Spirit.

Thank You for Your grace which is teaching me to trust myself and others. Thank You for life — life in all its abundance.

It was You Who gave me a desire to pray, and I am grateful for the prayer closet where we meet, and I thank You for Your Word. Life is exciting, and I am grateful that I am alive for such a time as this.

Thank You for past and present relationships. I learn from those who oppose me and from those who are for me. You taught me to recognize and understand my strengths and weaknesses. You gave me discernment and spiritual understanding. I enter Your gates with thanksgiving in my heart.

You are my Father. I am your child, loved by You unconditionally. I rejoice in You, Lord, and give thanks at the remembrance of Your holiness.

I am an overcomer by the blood of the Lamb, and by the word of my testimony.

In the name of Jesus, amen.

Scripture References

Psalm 100:1-5 AMP	Philippians 2:13
Psalm 92:1 AMP	Esther 4:14
Psalm 138:8	Psalm 100:4
Hebrews 13:15	Philippians 3:1
Genesis 50:20 NIV	Psalm 30:4
John 10:10	Revelation 12:11

II.
Prayer of Thanksgiving for Food Eaten While Traveling

Father, I ask for the wisdom to order that which is healthy and nourishing to my body.

In the name of Jesus, I resist the lust of the flesh and the lust of the eye as I scan the menu. When I am in doubt about what I am to order, I will pause and ask for wisdom which You will give generously without finding fault with me.

Should I unknowingly eat or drink any deadly thing, it will not harm me, for the Spirit of life makes me free from the law of sin and death.

Everything You have created, Father, is good, and nothing is to be thrown away or refused if it is received with thanksgiving. It is hallowed and consecrated by Your Word and by prayer.

I receive this food with thanksgiving and will eat the amount that is sufficient for me.

In the name of Jesus, amen.

Scripture References

James 1:5	Romans 8:2
1 John 2:16	1 Timothy 4:4,5 AMP
Mark 16:18	Psalm 136:1,25

Committing to a Fast

I.
Beginning a Fast
Introduction

There are different kinds of fasts: a total fast from foods and liquids for a short interval of time; a liquid fast, in which only water may be drunk; a juice fast, which involves drinking water and a given amount of juices at normal meal times; a fast from meats, in which only fruits and vegetables may be eaten.

It is important to understand the effects of fasting on the spirit, soul, and body. Before committing to a fast, I encourage you to study the Word of God and to read books that provide important nutritional and other health information. Understanding will help to avoid harm and injury — both physically and spiritually.

Do not flaunt your fast, but do talk with your family and close associates if necessary to let them know what you are doing.

(Personal note: During times of fasting I continue to prepare meals at home for my family.)

Prayer

Father, I consecrate this fast to You and set my mind to gain understanding in these matters for which I am concerned. *(Write your concerns out and keep them before your eyes. Do not lose sight of the reason for your fast.)*

I humble myself before You, Most High God. In accordance with Daniel 10:1-3, I will eat no _____ for the period of _____.

I obey the Words of Jesus by putting on festive clothing, so that no one will suspect that I am fasting.

Father, You know every secret, and I look to You for my reward. I am assured that You hear me when I pray according to Your will, and I know that I shall have the petitions that I desire of You.

Father, I delight myself in You, and You cause my desires to be agreeable with Your will.

I choose the fast which You have chosen: to loose the chains of injustice and untie the cords of the yoke, to set the oppressed free, and to break every yoke. I share my food with the hungry and provide the poor wanderer with shelter — when I see the naked, I will clothe him, and I will not turn away from my own flesh and blood. Then my light will break forth like the dawn, and my healing will quickly appear; then my righteousness will go before me, and Your glory, Lord, will be my rear guard.

Father, thank You for cleansing me — spirit, soul, and body. All my ways seem innocent to me, but my motives are weighed by You, my Lord and my Master. I commit this fast to You, and my plans will succeed. I thank You that it is You Who give the wise answer of the tongue.

Forever, O Lord, Your Word stands firm in heaven. Your faithfulness extends to every generation, like the earth You created; it endures by Your decree, for everything serves Your plans.

In Jesus' name, amen.

Scripture References

Matthew 6:17,18 TLB	1 Thessalonians 5:23
1 John 5:14,15	Proverbs 16:2,3 NIV
Psalm 37:4	Proverbs 16:1
Proverbs 16:3 AMP	Psalm 119:89-91 TLB
Isaiah 58:6-8 TLB	

II.
Ending a Fast

Introduction

It is best to break a fast by eating fruit, broth, or a light salad, gradually adding other foods day by day depending upon the length of the fast.

Prayer

Father, in the name of Jesus, You are my Light and my Salvation; whom shall I fear? You are the Strength of my life; of whom shall I be afraid?

Father, You have given me the desires of my heart. You have heard and answered my prayer. To You be the glory! Great things You have done!

I rest in You, awaiting the manifestation of all that I required and inquired of You.

I thank You for giving me Your strength to face each day full of sap [of spiritual vitality]. Today, I break this fast as You have directed. I thank You for this food because it is consecrated by Your Word and prayer.

In Jesus' name, amen.

Scripture References

Psalm 27:1	Psalm 92:14 AMP
Psalm 37:4	1 Timothy 4:4,5 AMP
Psalm 34:4 AMP	

Handling the Day of Trouble or Calamity

Introduction

During a time of trouble or calamity, it is some-times difficult to remember the promises of God. The pressures of the moment may seem overwhelming. At such times, it is often helpful to read, meditate, and pray the entire chapter of Psalm 91.

It may be that during a stressful time you will find this entire prayer too long. If so, draw from the Scriptures included in the following prayer. You may find yourself praying one paragraph, or reading it aloud to yourself or to your family and friends.

I also encourage you to meditate on this prayer during good times.

At all times, remember that faith comes by hearing, and hearing by the Word of God. (Rom. 10:17.)

Prayer

Father, I come to You in the name of Jesus, acknowledging You as my Refuge and High Tower. You are a refuge and a stronghold in these times of trouble (high cost, destitution, and desperation).

In the day of trouble You will hide me in Your shelter; in the secret place of Your tent will You hide me; You will set me high upon a rock. And now shall my head be lifted up above my enemies round about me; in Your tent I will offer sacrifices and shouting of joy; I will sing, yes, I will sing praises to You, O Lord. Hear, O Lord, when I cry aloud; have mercy and be gracious to me and answer me!

On the authority of Your Word, I declare that I have been made the righteousness of God in Christ Jesus. When I cry for help, You, Lord, hear me, and deliver me out of all my distress and troubles. You are close to me, for I am of a broken heart, and You save such as are crushed with sorrow for sin and are humbly and thoroughly penitent. Lord, many are the evils that confront me, but You deliver me out of them all.

Thank You for being merciful and gracious to me, O God, for my soul takes refuge and finds shelter and confidence in You; yes, in the shadow of Your wings I take refuge and am confident until calamities and destructive storms are passed. You perform on my behalf and reward me. You bring to pass Your purposes for me and surely You complete them!

Father, You are my Refuge and Strength [mighty and impenetrable to temptation], a very present and well-proved help in trouble.

Lord, You have given and bequeathed to me Your peace. By Your grace I will not let my heart be troubled, neither will I let it be afraid. With the help of the Holy Spirit I will [stop allowing myself to be agitated and disturbed; and I refuse to permit myself to be fearful and intimidated and cowardly and unsettled].

By faith, I respond to these troubles and calamities: [I am full of joy now!] I exult and triumph in my troubles and rejoice in my sufferings, knowing that pressure and affliction and hardship produce patient and unswerving endurance. And endurance (fortitude) develops maturity of character (approved faith and tried integrity). And character [of this sort] produces [the habit of] joyful and confident hope of eternal salvation.

Such hope never disappoints or deludes or shames me, for Your love has been poured out in my heart through the Holy Spirit Who has been given to me.

In Jesus name, amen.

Scripture References

Psalm 9:9 AMP	Psalm 57:1,2 AMP
Psalm 27:5-7 AMP	Psalm 46:1 AMP
2 Corinthians 5:21	John 14:27 AMP
Psalm 34:17-20 AMP	Romans 5:3-5 AMP

Breaking the Curse of Abuse

Introduction

**Christ redeemed us from the curse of the law
by becoming a curse for us, for it is written:
"Cursed is everyone who is hung on a tree."**

Galatians 3:13 NIV

On a Sunday morning after I had taught a lesson titled "Healing for the Emotionally Wounded," a young man wanted to speak with me. I listened intently as he told me that he had just been released from jail and was now on probation for physically abusing his family. His wife had filed for divorce, and he was living alone. It was not easy for him to confess his sin to me, and I was impressed by his humble attitude.

He said, "I am glad that this message is being given in the Church, and the abused can receive ministry. Is there anywhere that the abuser can go to receive spiritual help?"

He shared with me that he was attending a support group for abusers. He desired to commit to a church where he could receive forgiveness and acceptance. He knew that any lasting change would have to be from the inside out by the Spirit. I prayed with him, but it would be three years before I could write a prayer for the abuser.

As I read, studied, and sought the Lord, I discovered that the abuser is usually a person who has been abused. Often, the problem is a generational curse that has been in the family of the abuser for as far back as anyone can remember. Many times the abuser declares that he will never treat his wife and children as he has been treated, but in spite of his resolve he finds himself reacting in the same violent manner.

The generational curse is reversed as the abuser is willing to allow God to remove the character flaws that have held him in bondage.

If you are an abuser, I encourage you to pray this prayer for yourself until it becomes a reality in your life.

If you know someone who is an abuser, pray this as a prayer of intercession in the third person.

Prayer

I receive and confess that Jesus is my Lord, and I ask that Your will be done in my life.

Father, You have rescued me from the dominion of darkness and have brought me into the Kingdom of the Son of Your love. Once I was darkness, but now I am light in You; I walk as a child of light. The abuse is exposed and reproved by the light, it is made visible and clear; and where everything is visible and clear there is light.

Help me to grow in grace (undeserved favor, spiritual strength) and recognition and knowledge and understanding of my Lord and Savior, Jesus Christ, so that I may experience Your love and trust You to be a Father to me.

The history of my earthly family is filled with abusive behavior, much hatred, strife, and rage. The painful memory of past abuse *(verbal, emotional, physical, and/or sexual)* has caused me to be hostile and abusive to others.

I desire to be a doer of the Word, and not a hearer only. No matter which way I turn, I can't make myself do right. I want to, but I can't. When I want to do good, I don't; and when I try not to do wrong, I do it anyway. It seems that sin still has me in its evil grasp. This pain has caused me to hurt myself and others. In my mind I want to be Your willing servant, but instead I find myself still enslaved to sin.

I confess my sin of abuse, resentment, and hostility toward others, and I ask You to forgive me. You are faithful and just to forgive my sin and cleanse me from all unrighteousness. I am tired of reliving the past in my present life, perpetuating the generational curse of anger and abuse.

Jesus was made a curse for me; therefore, Lord, I put on Your whole armor that I may be able to success- fully stand against all the strategies and the tricks of the devil. I thank You that the evil power of abuse is broken, overthrown, and cast down. I submit myself to You and resist the devil. The need to hurt others no longer controls me or my family.

In Jesus' name, amen.

Scripture References

Romans 10:9	Romans 7:18-25 TLB
Matthew 6:10	1 John 1:9
Colossians 1:13 AMP	Galatians 3:13
Ephesians 5:8,13 AMP	Ephesians 6:11,12 TLB
2 Peter 3:18 AMP	2 Corinthians 10:5
James 1:22	James 4:7

Healing From Abuse

Introduction

This prayer can be applied to any form of abuse —
physical, mental, emotional, or sexual. I wrote it after
reading T. D. Jakes' book, *Woman, Thou Art Loosed*.[1] By
praying it, I personally have experienced victory and
freedom — I am no longer a victim but an overcomer.

Prayer

Lord, You are my High Priest, and I ask You to
loose me from this "infirmity." The abuse I suffered
pronounced me guilty and condemned. I was bound —
in an emotional prison — crippled, and could in no
wise lift up myself. You have called me to Yourself, and
I have come.

The anointing that is upon You is present to bind
up and heal the brokenness and emotional wounds of
the past. You are the Truth that makes me free.

Thank You, Lord, for guiding me through the
steps to emotional wholeness. You have begun a good

work in me, and You will perform it until the day of Christ Jesus.

Father, I desire to live according to the Spirit of life in Christ Jesus. This Spirit of life in Christ, like a strong wind, has magnificently cleared the air, freeing me from a fated lifetime of brutal tyranny at the hands of abuse.

Since I am now free, it is my desire to forget those things that lie behind and strain forward to what lies ahead. I press on toward the goal to win the [supreme and heavenly] prize to which You in Christ Jesus are calling me upward. The past will no longer control my thinking patterns or my behavior.

Praise be to You! I am a new creature in Christ Jesus. Old things have passed away; and, behold, all things have become new. I declare and decree that henceforth I will walk in newness of life.

Forgive me, Father, for self-hatred and self-condemnation. I am Your child. You sent Jesus that I

---

[1](Shippensburg, PA: Treasure House, 1993).

might have life and have it more abundantly. Thank You for the blood of Jesus that makes me whole.

It is my desire to throw all spoiled virtue and cancerous evil in the garbage. In simple humility, I let my Gardener, You Lord, landscape me with the Word, making a salvation-garden of my life.

Father, by Your grace, I forgive my abuser/abusers and ask You to bring him/her/them to repentance.

In the name of Jesus I pray, amen.

Scripture References

Luke 13:11,12	Romans 6:4
John 14:6	1 John 3:1,2
John 8:32	John 10:10
Philippians 1:6	1 John 1:7
Romans 8:2 MESSAGE	James 1:21 MESSAGE
Philippians 3:13,14 AMP	Matthew 5:44
2 Corinthians 5:17	2 Peter 3:9

Letting Go of the Past

Father, I realize my helplessness in saving myself, and I glory in what Christ Jesus has done for me. I let go — put aside all past sources of my confidence — counting them worth less than nothing, in order that I may experience Christ and become one with Him.

Lord, I have received Your Son, and He has given me the authority (power, privilege, and right) to become Your child.

I unfold my past and put into proper perspective those things that are behind. I have been crucified with Christ, and I no longer live, but Christ lives in me. The life I live in the body, I live by faith in the Son of God, Who loved me and gave Himself for me. I trust in You, Lord, with all my heart and lean not on my own understanding. In all my ways I acknowledge You, and You will make my paths straight.

I want to know Christ and the power of His resurrection and the fellowship of sharing in His sufferings, becoming like Him in His death, and so, somehow, to attain to the resurrection from the dead. So, whatever it takes, I will be one who lives in the fresh newness of life of those who are alive from the dead.

I don't mean to say that I am perfect. I haven't learned all I should even yet, but I keep working toward that day when I will finally be all that Christ saved me for and wants me to be.

I am bringing all my energies to bear on this one thing: regardless of my past I look forward to what lies ahead. I strain to reach the end of the race and receive the prize for which You are calling me up to heaven because of what Christ Jesus did for me.

In His name I pray, amen.

Scripture References

Philippians 3:7-9 TLB   Proverbs 3:5,6 NIV

John 1:12 AMP   Philippians 3:10,11 NIV

Psalm 32:5 AMP   Romans 6:4

Philippians 3:13   Philippians 3:12-14 TLB

Galatians 2:20 NIV

Strength To Overcome Cares and Burdens

Why are you cast down, O my inner self? And why should you moan over me and be disquieted within me?

Father, You set Yourself against the proud and haughty, but give grace [continually] unto the humble. I submit myself therefore to You, God. In the name of Jesus, I resist the devil, and he will flee from me. I resist the cares of the world which try to pressure me daily. Except the Lord builds the house, they labor in vain who build it.

Jesus, I come to You, for I labor and am heavyladen and over burdened, and You cause me to rest — You will ease and relieve and refresh my soul.

I take Your Yoke upon me, and I learn of You; for You are gentle (meek) and humble (lowly) in heart, and I will find rest — relief, ease and refreshment and recreation and blessed quiet — for my soul. For Your yoke is wholesome *(easy)* — not harsh, hard, sharp or pressing, but comfortable, gracious and pleasant; and Your burden is light and easy to be borne.

I cast my burden on You, Lord, [releasing the weight of it] and You will sustain me; I thank You that You will never allow me, the [consistently] righteous, to be moved — made to slip, fall or fail.

In the name of Jesus, I withstand the devil. I am firm in my faith [against his onset] — rooted, established, strong, immovable and determined. I cease from [the weariness and pain] of human labor; and am zealous and exert myself and strive diligently to enter into the rest [of God] — to know and experience it for myself.

Father, I thank You that Your presence goes with me, and that You give me rest. I am still and rest in You, Lord; I wait for You, and patiently stay myself upon You. I will not fret myself, nor shall I let my heart be troubled, neither shall I let it be afraid. I hope in You, God, and wait expectantly for You; for I shall yet praise You, for You are the help of my countenance, and my God.

In Jesus' name, amen.

Scripture References (AMP)

Psalm 42:11a
James 4:6,7
Psalm 127:1a
Matthew 11:28-30
Psalm 55:22
1 Peter 5:9a

Hebrews 4:10b,11
Exodus 33:14
Psalm 37:7
John 14:27b
Psalm 42:11b

Renewing the Mind

Father, in Jesus' name, I thank You that I shall prosper and be in health, even as my soul prospers. I have the mind of Christ, the Messiah, and do hold the thoughts (feelings and purposes) of His heart. I trust in You, Lord, with all my heart; I lean not unto my own understanding but in all my ways I acknowledge You, and You shall direct my paths.

Today I submit myself to Your Word which exposes and sifts and analyzes and judges the very thoughts and purposes of my heart. (For the weapons of my warfare are not carnal, but mighty through You to the pulling down of strongholds — *intimidation, fears, doubts, unbelief and failure*.) I refute arguments and theories and reasonings and every proud and lofty thing that sets itself up against the (true) knowledge of God; and I lead every thought and purpose away captive into the obedience of Christ the Messiah, the Anointed One.

Today I shall be transformed by the renewing of my mind, that I may prove what is that good and acceptable and perfect will of God. Your Word, Lord, shall not depart out of my mouth; but I shall meditate on it day and night, that I may observe to do according to all that is written therein: for then I shall make my way prosperous, then I shall have good success.

My thoughts are the thoughts of the diligent which tend only to plenteousness. Therefore I will not fret or have any anxiety about anything, but in everything by prayer and petition [definite requests] with thanksgiving continue to make my wants known unto You, Lord. And Your peace which transcends all understanding, shall garrison and mount guard over my heart and mind in Christ Jesus.

Today I fix my mind on whatever is *true*, whatever is *worthy* of *reverence* and is *honorable* and *seemly*, whatever is *just*, whatever is *pure*, whatever is *lovely* and *lovable*, whatever is *kind* and *winsome* and *gracious*. If there is any *virtue* and *excellence*, if there is anything *worthy* of *praise*, I will think on and weigh and take account of these things.

Today I roll my works upon You, Lord — I commit and trust them wholly to You; [You will cause my thoughts to become agreeable to Your will, and] so shall my plans be established and succeed.

In Jesus' name I pray, amen.

Scripture References

3 John 2

1 Corinthians 2:16b AMP

Proverbs 3:5,6

Hebrews 4:12b AMP

2 Corinthians 10:4

2 Corinthians 10:5 AMP

Romans 12:2

Joshua 1:8

Proverbs 21:5a

Philippians 4:6-8 AMP

Proverbs 16:3 AMP

Conquering the Thought Life

In the name of Jesus, I take authority over my thought life. Even though I walk (live) in the flesh, I am not carrying on my warfare according to the flesh and using mere human weapons. For the weapons of my warfare are not physical (weapons of flesh and blood), but they are mighty before God for the overthrow and destruction of strongholds. I refute arguments and theories and reasonings and every proud and lofty thing that sets itself up against the (true) knowledge of God; and I lead every thought and purpose away captive into the obedience of Christ, the Messiah, the Anointed One.

With my soul I will bless the Lord with every thought and purpose in life. My mind will not wander out of the presence of God. My life shall glorify the Father — *spirit, soul, and body*. I take no account of the evil done to me — I pay no attention to a suffered wrong. It holds no place in my thought life. I am ever ready to believe the best of every person. I gird up the loins of my mind, and I set my mind and keep it set on what is above — the higher things — not on the things that are on the earth.

Whatever is true, whatever is worthy of reverence and is honorable and seemly, whatever is just, whatever is pure, whatever is lovely and lovable, whatever is kind and winsome and gracious, if there is any virtue and excellence, if there is anything worthy of praise, I will think on and weigh and take account of these things — I will fix my mind on them.

The carnal mind is no longer operative for I have the mind of Christ, the Messiah, and do hold the thoughts (feelings and purposes) of His heart. In the name of Jesus, I will practice what I have learned and received and heard and seen in Christ, and model my way of living on it, and the God of peace — of untroubled, undisturbed well-being — will be with me.

In Jesus' name, amen.

Scripture References (AMP)

2 Corinthians 10:3-5   Colossians 3:2
Psalm 103:1   Philippians 4:8

1 Corinthians 6:20   1 Corinthians 2:16
1 Corinthians 13:5b,7a Philippians 4:9
1 Peter 1:13

Casting Down Imaginations

Father, though I live in the world, I do not wage war as the world does. The weapons I fight with are not the weapons of the world. On the contrary, they have divine power to demolish strongholds. I demolish arguments and every pretension that sets itself up against the knowledge of You, and I take captive every thought to make it obedient to Christ.

In the name of Jesus, I ask You, Father, to bless those who have despitefully used me. Whenever I feel afraid, I will trust in You. When I feel miserable, I will express thanksgiving, and when I feel that life is unfair, I will remember that You are more than enough.

When I feel ashamed, help me to remember that I no longer have to be afraid; I will not suffer shame. I am delivered from the fear of disgrace; I will not be humiliated. I relinquish the shame of my youth.

It is well with my soul for You have redeemed me. You have called me by my name.

I am in Your will for my life at this time. I am being transformed through the renewing of my mind. I am able to test and approve [for myself] what Your will is — Your good and acceptable and perfect will.

You have good things reserved for my future. All my needs will be met according to Your riches in glory. I will replace worry for my family by asking You to protect and care for them.

You are love, and perfect love casts out fear.

In Jesus' name, amen.

Scripture References

2 Corinthians 10:3-5 NIV	Romans 12:2 AMP
Luke 6:28	Jeremiah 29:11 AMP
Isaiah 54:4 NIV	Philippians 4:19
Isaiah 43:1	1 Peter 5:7
Romans 12:2	1 John 4:8,18

Victory Over Gluttony

Father, it is written in Your Word that if I confess with my lips that Jesus is Lord and believe in my heart that You have raised Him from the dead, I shall be saved. Father, I am Your child and confess that Jesus Christ is Lord over my spirit, my soul, and my body. I make Him Lord over every situation in my life. Therefore, I can do all things through Christ Jesus who strengthens me.

Father, *I have made a quality decision to give You my appetite.* I choose *Jesus* rather than the indulgence of my flesh. I command my body to get in line with Your Word. I eat only as much as is sufficient for me. I eat and am satisfied.

When I sit down to eat, I consider what is before me. I am not given to the desire of dainties or deceitful foods.

Like a boxer, I buffet my body — handle it roughly, discipline it by hardships — and subdue it. I bring my body into subjection to my spirit man — the inward man — the real me. Not all things are helpful — good for me to do though permissible. I will not become the slave of anything or be brought under its power.

My body is for the Lord. I dedicate my body presenting all my members and faculties — as a living sacrifice, holy and well pleasing to You, presenting them as implements of righteousness. I am united to You, Lord, and become one spirit with You. My body is the temple, the very sanctuary, of the Holy Spirit Who lives within me, Whom I have received as a gift from You, Father.

I am not my own. I was bought for a price, made Your own. So then, I honor You and bring glory to You in my body. Therefore, I always exercise and discipline myself, bringing under authority my carnal affections, bodily appetites, and worldly desires. I endeavor in all respects to have a clean conscience, void of offense toward You, Father, and toward men. I keep myself from idols — from anything and everything that would occupy the place in my heart due to You, from any sort of substitute for You that would take first place in my life.

I no longer spend the rest of my natural life living by my human appetites and desires, but I live for what You will! I am on my guard. I refuse to be overburdened and depressed, weighed down with the giddiness and headache and nausea of self-indulgence, drunkenness (on food), worldly worries and cares, for I have been given a spirit of power and of love and of a sound mind. I have discipline and self-control.

Father, I *do* resist temptation in the name of Jesus. I strip off and throw aside every encumbrance — unnecessary weight — and this gluttony which so readily tries to cling to and entangle me. I run with patient endurance and steady persistence the appointed course of the race that is set before me, looking away from all distractions to Jesus, the author and finisher of my faith.

Christ the Messiah *will* be magnified and get glory and praise in this body of mine and *will* be boldly exalted in my person. Thank You, Father, in Jesus' name! Hallelujah! Amen.

Scripture References

Romans 10:9,10	Romans 6:13
Philippians 4:13	1 Corinthians 9:27 AMP
Deuteronomy 30:19	1 Corinthians 6:19,20 AMP
Romans 13:14	Romans 12:1 AMP
Proverbs 25:16	Luke 21:34 AMP
2 Timothy 1:7 AMP	1 Corinthians 6:12,13,17 AMP
Proverbs 23:1-3	James 4:7
Hebrews 12:1,2 AMP	Philippians 1:20 AMP

Victory Over Fear

Father, in Jesus' name, I confess and believe that no weapon formed against me shall prosper, and any tongue that rises against me in judgment I shall show to be in the wrong. I believe I dwell in the secret place of the Most High. I shall remain stable and fixed under the shadow of the Almighty God Whose power no foe can withstand — this secret place hides me from the strife of tongues.

I believe the wisdom of God's Word dwells in me, and because it does, I realize that I am without fear or dread of evil. In all my ways I know and acknowledge God and His Word; thus, He directs and makes straight and plain my pathway. As I attend to God's Word, it is health to my nerves and sinews, and marrow and moistening to my bones.

I am strengthened and reinforced with mighty power in my innerself by the Holy Spirit Himself Who dwells in me. God is my strength and my refuge, and I confidently trust in Him and in His Word. I am empowered through my union with Almighty God. This gives me the superhuman, supernatural strength to walk in divine health and to live in abundance.

God Himself has said, "I will never leave you without support or forsake you or let you down, my child. [I will] not, [I will] not, [I will] not in any degree leave you helpless or relax my hold on you...assuredly not!" (based on Hebrews 13:5 AMP).

I take comfort and am encouraged and confidently and boldly say, "The Lord is my helper. I will not be seized with alarm. I will not fear or be terrified, for what can man do to me?"

I confess and believe that my children are disciples taught of the Lord and obedient to God's will. Great is the peace and undisturbed composure of my children — because God Himself contends with that which contends with me and my children, and He gives them safety and eases them. God will perfect that which concerns me.

This Word of God that I have spoken is alive and full of power. It is active and operative. It energizes me, and it affects me. As I speak God's Word, it is sharper than any two-edged sword, and it is penetrating into my joints and into the marrow of my bones. It is healing to my flesh. It is prosperity for me. It is the magnificent Word of Almighty God. According to His Word that I have spoken, so be it! Hallelujah! Amen.

Scripture References

Isaiah 54:17 AMP	Ephesians 6:10 AMP
Psalm 91:1 AMP	Hebrews 13:5,6 AMP
Psalm 31:20	Isaiah 54:13 AMP
Proverbs 3:6,8 AMP	Isaiah 49:25 AMP
Ephesians 3:16 AMP	Psalm 138:8 AMP
Psalm 91:2	Hebrews 4:12 AMP

Overcoming a Feeling of Abandonment

Introduction

**When my father and my mother forsake me,
then the Lord will take me up.**

Psalm 27:10

This prayer was prompted by a letter I received from someone who is incarcerated. According to his letter, he grew up in a family of fighters and felt abandoned by his family and so-called friends. His pugnacious attitude controlled him, and eventually his aggressive temperament caused him to almost kill someone.

In prison he was ridiculed and harassed by inmates who encouraged him to fight. His wife divorced him, and again he was left alone. Thoughts that "no one likes me" continually tormented him, but he desired to know how to change his thinking.

A laborer of the harvest introduced him to Jesus and my book, *Prayers That Avail Much, Volume 1*.[1] He

---

[1]Tulsa: Harrison House, 1989.

still had trouble controlling his temper even with those who might have been his friends. His letter was filled with the pain of loneliness and abandonment. The following is a revised and expanded version of the original prayer I wrote encouraging him to pray for himself.

Prayer

Father, I have confessed Jesus as my Lord and believe in my heart that You raised Him from the dead. I ask for the power of the Holy Spirit to overcome the resentment I feel towards those who abused and abandoned me.

Now, I am Your child. When other people leave me and I feel unloved, I am thankful that You will never, ever leave me alone or reject me.

Jesus gave His life for me and called me His friend. He lives in my heart, and I am on my way to heaven. That is plenty to be thankful for. So when I am lonely or discouraged, I can think of things that are pure, and holy, and good, even when I am apart from everyone.

Heavenly Father, I ask You to strengthen me and help me while in the presence of the dangers surrounding me. You have assigned angels who will accompany, defend, and preserve me in all my ways [of obedience and service]. I am not alone. Your Word says that there is nothing that can separate me from the love of Christ — not pain, nor stress, nor persecution. I will come to the top of every circumstance or trial through Jesus' love.

You are concerned with the smallest detail that concerns me, and You are my Help. I ask You for friends who will admonish and encourage me. Teach me how to trust others and be a friend who sticks closer than a brother. Help me to walk in Your love and show myself friendly.

In Jesus' name, amen.

Scripture References

Romans 10:9,10 NIV

Hebrews 13:5 NIV

John 15:13-15 NIV

1 Thessalonians 5:18 TLB

Philippians 4:8 TLB

Isaiah 41:10 TLB

Psalm 91:11 AMP

Romans 8:35,39

Psalm 138:8 AMP

Psalm 46:1 MESSAGE

Proverbs 18:24

Overcoming Discouragement

Introduction

> Moses returned to the Lord and said, "O
> Lord, why have you brought trouble upon this
> people? Is this why you sent me? Ever since I
> went to Pharaoh to speak in your name, he has
> brought trouble upon this people, and you have
> not rescued your people at all."
>
> Exodus 5:22,23 NIV

Here in this passage, we find Moses discouraged,
complaining to God.

It is important that we approach God with integrity
in an attitude of humility. Because we fear making a
negative confession, we sometimes cross the line of
honesty into the line of denial and delusion.

Let's be honest. God already knows what we are
feeling. He can handle our anger, complaints, and disap-
pointments. He understands us. He is aware of our
human frailties (Ps. 103:14) and can be touched with
the feelings of our infirmities. (Heb. 4:15.)

Whether your "trouble" is a business failure, abandonment, depression, mental disorder, chemical imbalance, oppression, a marriage problem, a child who is in a strange land of drugs and alcohol, financial disaster, or anything else, the following prayer is for you.

Sometimes when you are in the midst of discouragement it is difficult to remember that you have ever known any Scripture. I admonish you to read this prayer aloud until you recognize the reality of God's Word in your spirit, soul, and body. Remember, God is watching over His Word to perform it. (Jer. 1:12 AMP.) He will perfect that which concerns you. (Ps. 138:8.)

Prayer

Lord, I do not understand why You have allowed this trouble to assail me. It was after I began to follow You in obedience that this trouble was manifested in my life. I have exhausted all my possibilities for changing my situation and circumstances and have found that I am powerless to change. I believe; help me overcome my unbelief. All things are not possible with man, but all things are possible with You. I humble myself before You, and You will lift me up.

I have a great High Priest Who has gone through the heavens, Jesus Your Son, and I hold firmly to the faith I profess. My High Priest is able to sympathize with my weaknesses. He was tempted in every way, just as I am — yet was without sin. I approach Your throne of grace with confidence, so that I may receive mercy and find grace to help me in my time of need.

In the face of discouragement, disappointment, and anger, I choose to believe that Your word to Moses is Your word to me. You are mighty to deliver. Because of Your mighty hand, You will drive out the forces that have set themselves up against me. You are the Lord, Yahweh, the Promise-Keeper, the Almighty One. You appeared to Abraham, to Isaac, and to Jacob and established Your covenant with them.

Father, I believe that You have heard my groaning, my cries. I will live to see Your promises of deliverance fulfilled in my life. You have not forgotten one word of Your promise; You are a Covenant-Keeper.

It is You Who will bring me out from under the yoke of bondage and free me from being a slave to _____. You have redeemed me with an outstretched arm and with mighty acts of judgment. You have taken me as Your own, and You are my God. You are a Father to me. You have delivered me from the past that has held me in bondage and translated me into the Kingdom of love, peace, joy, and righteousness. I will no longer settle for the pain of the past. Where sin abounds, grace does much more abound.

Father, what You have promised, I will go and possess, in the name of Jesus. I am willing to take the chance, to take the risk, to get back into the good fight of faith. It is with patient endurance and steady and active persistence that I run the race, the appointed course that is set before me. I rebuke the spirit of fear for I am established in righteousness. Oppression and destruction shall not come near me. Behold, they may gather together and stir up strife, but it is not from You, Father. Whoever stirs up strife against me shall fall and surrender to me. I am more than a conqueror through Him Who loves me.

In His name I pray, amen.

Scripture References

(This prayer is based on Exodus 5:22-6:11
and includes other verses where applicable.)

Mark 9:24 NIV	Deuteronomy 26:8
Luke 18:27	Colossians 1:13
1 Peter 5:6 NIV	Romans 5:20
Hebrews 4:14-16 NIV	1 Timothy 6:12
Exodus 6:3,4 AMP	Hebrews 12:1 AMP
Genesis 49:22-26 AMP	Isaiah 54:14-16
1 Kings 8:56	Romans 8:37

Overcoming Intimidation

Father, I come to You in the name of Jesus, confessing that intimidation has caused me to stumble. I ask Your forgiveness for thinking of myself as inferior, for I am created in your image, and I am Your workmanship. Jesus said that the Kingdom of God is in me. Therefore, the power that raised Jesus from the dead dwells in me and causes me to face life with hope and divine energy.

The Lord is my light and my salvation; whom shall I fear? The Lord is the strength of my life; of whom shall I be afraid? Lord, You said that You would never leave me or forsake me. Therefore, I can say without any doubt or fear that You are my helper, and I am not afraid of anything that mere man can do to me. Greater is He Who is in me than he who is in the world. If God is for me, who can be against me? I am free from the fear of man and public opinion.

Father, You have not given me a spirit of timidity — of cowardice, of craven and cringing and fawning fear —

but You have given me a spirit of power and of love and of a calm and well-balanced mind and discipline and self-control. I can do all things through Christ Who gives me the strength. Amen.

Scripture References

1 John 1:9	Ephesians 2:10
Luke 17:21	Ephesians 1:19,20
Colossians 1:29	Psalm 1:27
Hebrews 13:5	1 John 4:4
Romans 3:31	Proverbs 29:25
2 Timothy 1:7	Philippians 4:13

Overcoming a Sense of Hopelessness

Father, as Your child I boldly come before Your throne of grace that I may receive mercy and find grace to help in this time of need.

Father, I know that Your ears are open to my prayers. I ask that You listen to my prayer, O God, and hide not Yourself from my supplication! I ask that You attend to me and answer me, for I am restless and distraught in my complaint and must moan. Fear and trembling have come upon me; horror and fright have overwhelmed me.

Oh, that I had wings like a dove! I would fly away and be at rest. Yes, I would wander far away, I would lodge in the wilderness. I would hasten to escape and to find a shelter from the stormy wind and tempest.

I am calling upon You, my God, to rescue me. You redeem my life in peace from the battle of hopelessness that is against me. I cast my burden on You, Lord, [releasing the weight of it] and You sustain me; You will never allow the [consistently] righteous to be moved (made to slip, fall, or fail).

Hopelessness lies in wait for me to swallow me up or trample me all day long. What time I am afraid, I will have confidence in and put my trust and reliance in You. By [Your help], God, I will praise Your Word; on You I lean, rely, and confidently put my trust; I will not fear.

You know my every sleepless night. Each tear and heartache is answered with Your promise. I am thanking You with all my heart. You pulled me from the brink of death, my feet from the cliff-edge of doom. Now, I stroll at leisure with You in the sunlit fields of life.

[What, what would have become of me], Lord, had I not believed that I would see Your goodness in the land of the living! I wait and hope for and expect You; I am brave and of good courage, and I let my heart be stout and enduring. Yes, I wait for and hope for and expect You.

Father, I give You all my worries and cares, for You are always thinking about me and watching everything that concerns me. I am well balanced and careful — vigilant, watching out for attacks from Satan, my great enemy. By Your grace I am standing firm, trusting You, and I remember that other Christians all around the world are going through these sufferings too. You, God, are full of kindness through Christ and will give me Your eternal glory.

In the name of Jesus I am an overcomer by the blood of the Lamb, and by the word of my testimony. Amen.

Scripture References

Hebrews 4:16

Psalm 55:1 MESSAGE

Psalm 55:1,2 AMP

Psalm 55:5-8 AMP

Psalm 55:16,18,22 AMP

Psalm 56:2-4 AMP

Psalm 56:5,8 MESSAGE

Psalm 56:13 MESSAGE

Psalm 27:13,14 AMP

1 Peter 5:7-9 AMP, TLB

Revelation 12:11

Overcoming a Feeling of Rejection

Introduction

Rejection seems to create an identity crisis. Rejection by those in the Body of Christ is especially cruel, but it happens more often than it should. When you are thrown into an identity crisis, you have the opportunity to erase old tapes which have played in your mind for a long time, and replace those self-destructive thoughts with God-thoughts.

Your heavenly Father saw you and approved of you even while you were in your mother's womb. (Ps. 139:13-16.) He gave you survival tools that would bring you to the place where you are today. He is a Father Who has been waiting for you to come home to truth — the truth that will set you free. (John 8:32.)

Future rejection may hurt, but it will be only for a season. (1 Pet. 1:6.) The Word of God is your shield against all the fiery darts of the devil. (Eph. 6:16,17.)

For victory over your feeling of rejection, pray the following prayer in faith and joy.[1]

Prayer

Lord, Your Son Jesus is my High Priest. He understands and sympathizes with my weaknesses and this excruciating pain of rejection. In His name I approach Your throne of grace with confidence, so that I may receive mercy and find grace to help me in my time of need. I ask You to forgive my sins, and I receive Your mercy; I expect Your healing grace to dispel the rejection I am suffering because of the false accusations and demeaning actions of another.

Father, Jesus was despised and rejected — a man of sorrows, acquainted with bitterest grief. The grief of _____ turning against me and treating me as an outcast is consuming me, just as my rejection consumed Your Son Who freely gave His life for me.

---

[1] For further support, I encourage you to read Psalm 27 and the book of Ephesians in their entirety.

Forgive me for turning my back on Jesus and looking the other way — He was despised, and I didn't care. Yet it was my grief He bore, my sorrows that weighed Him down. He was wounded and bruised for my sins. He was beaten that I might have peace; He was lashed — and with His stripes I was healed.

In the face of rejection I will declare, **The Lord is my Light and my Salvation — whom shall I fear or dread? The Lord is the Refuge and Stronghold of my life — of whom shall I be afraid?** (Ps. 27:1 AMP.)

I know right from wrong and cherish Your laws in my heart: I won't be afraid of people's scorn or their slanderous talk. Slanderous talk is temporal and fades away. Your Word will never pass away.

Father, I choose to look at the things which are eternal; Your justice and mercy shall last forever, and Your salvation from generation to generation. Your eyes are upon me, for I have right standing with You, and Your ears are attentive to my prayer. You spoke to me, and asked, "Now who is going to hurt you if you are a zealous follower of that which is good?"

In my heart I set Christ apart as holy [and acknowledge Him] as Lord. I am always ready to give a logical defense to anyone who asks me to account for the hope that is in me, but I do it courteously and respectfully. I purpose [to see to it that] my conscience is entirely clear (unimpaired), so that, when I am falsely accused as an evildoer, those who threaten me abusively and revile my right behavior in Christ may come to be ashamed [of slandering my good life].

There is wonderful joy ahead, even though the going is rough for a while down here. These trials are only to test my faith, to see whether or not it is strong and pure. It is being tested as fire tests gold and purifies it — and my faith is far more precious to You, Lord, than mere gold; so if my faith remains strong after being tried in the test tube of fiery trials, it will bring me much praise and glory and honor on the day of Jesus' return.

In spite of the rejection I have experienced, I declare that everything You say about me in Your Word is true:

I am blessed with all spiritual blessings in heavenly places in Christ. (Eph. 1:3.)

I am chosen by You, my Father. (Eph. 1:4.)

I am holy and without blame. (Eph. 1:4.)

I am Your child according to the good pleasure of Your will. (Eph. 1:5.)

I am accepted in the Beloved. (Eph. 1:6.)

I am redeemed through the blood of Jesus. (Eph. 1:7.)

I am a person of wisdom and prudence. (Eph. 1:8.)

I am an heir. (Eph. 1:11.)

I have a spirit of wisdom and revelation in the knowledge of Christ. (Eph. 1:17.)

I am saved by Your grace. (Eph. 2:5.)

I am seated in heavenly places in Christ Jesus. (Eph. 2:6.)

I am Your workmanship. (Eph. 2:10.)

I am near to You by the blood of Christ. (Eph. 2:13.)

I am a new creation. (Eph. 2:15.)

I am of Your household. (Eph. 2:19.)

I am a citizen of heaven. (Eph. 2:19.)

I am a partaker of Your promises in Christ. (2 Pet. 1:4.)

I am strengthened with might by Your Spirit. (Eph. 3:16.)

I allow Christ to dwell in my heart by faith. (Eph. 3:17.)

I am rooted and grounded in love. (Eph. 3:17.)

I speak the truth in love. (Eph. 4:15.)

I am renewed in the spirit of my mind. (Eph. 4:23.)

I am Your follower. (Eph. 5:1.)

I walk in love. (Eph. 5:2.)

I am light in You. (Eph. 5:8.)

I walk circumspectly. (Eph. 5:15.)

I am filled with the Spirit. (Eph. 5:18.)

I am more than a conqueror. (Rom. 8:37.)

I am an overcomer. (Rev. 12:11.)

I am Your righteousness in Christ Jesus. (1 Cor. 1:30.)

I am healed. (1 Pet. 2:24.)

I am free. (John 8:36.)

I am salt. (Matt. 5:13.)

I am consecrated. (1 Cor. 6:11 AMP.)

I am sanctified. (1 Cor. 6:11.)

I am victorious. (1 John 5:4.)

Everything You say about me is true, Lord.

In Your name I pray, amen.

Scripture References

Hebrews 4:14-16 NIV   Isaiah 51:7,8 TLB

Isaiah 53:3-5 TLB   1 Peter 3:12-17 AMP

2 Corinthians 4:18   1 Peter 1:6,7 TLB

Overcoming Worry

Father, I depart from evil and do good. I seek, inquire for, and crave peace. I pursue (go after) it! When my ways please You, Lord, You make even my enemies to be at peace with me.

Lord, You have given to me Your peace; Your [own] peace You have bequeathed to me. It is not the peace that the world gives. I will not let my heart be troubled, neither will I let it be afraid. [I refuse to be agitated and disturbed; and I will not permit myself to be fearful and intimidated and cowardly and unsettled.]

Instead of worrying, I will pray. I will let petitions and praises shape my worries into prayers, letting You, Father, know my concerns, not forgetting to thank You for the answers. Your peace will keep my thoughts and my heart quiet and at rest as I trust in Christ Jesus, my Lord. It is wonderful what happens when Christ displaces worry at the center of my life.

Thank You for guarding me and keeping me in perfect and constant peace. My mind [both its inclination and its character] is stayed on You. I commit myself to You, lean on You, and hope confidently in You.

I let the peace (soul harmony which comes) from Christ rule (act as umpire continually) in my heart [deciding and settling with finality all questions that arise in my mind]. I am thankful (appreciative), [giving praise to You always].

In Jesus' name, amen.

Scripture References

Philippians 4:6,7   Colossians 3:15 AMP
    MESSAGE, TLB   Proverbs 16:7 AMP
Psalm 34:14 AMP   John 14:27 AMP
Isaiah 26:3 AMP

Overcoming Hypersensitivity

Introduction

A new command I give you: Love one
another. As I have loved you, so you must love
one another. By this all men will know that you
are my disciples, if you love one another.

John 13:34 NIV

The royal law of love is the counter-agent for
hypersensitivity.

First Corinthians 13:5 AMP reveals that love ...is
not conceited (arrogant and inflated with pride); it is
not rude (unmannerly) and does not act unbecomingly.
Love (God's love in us) does not insist on its own rights
or its own way, for it is not self-seeking; it is not touchy
or fretful or resentful; it takes no account of evil done to
it [it pays no attention to a suffered wrong].

An overly sensitive person is thin-skinned, and
experiences feelings of alienation, irritability, and resentment in relationships.

The hypersensitive person has usually experienced deep hurt from rejection and needs a lot of approval from others. This individual is excessively sensitive to remarks that may or may not be intended to be hurtful. It is difficult for a person of this nature to trust others, to accept constructive criticism or advice, and this weakness hinders positive relationships. When presentations or suggestions are rejected, that action is taken as a personal attack.

Hypersensitivity is an enemy that can be overcome through spiritual warfare. In waging the good warfare, we have God-given weapons to overthrow our adversary. These weapons include among other things: the anointing that is upon Jesus to bind up and heal the broken-hearted (Luke 4:18), the sword of the Spirit, which is the Word of God (Eph. 6:17), the shield of faith (Eph. 6:16), and the help of the Holy Spirit (John 14:16 AMP), which may come through a Christian counselor, a minister, or a friend.

James instructed us, **Confess to one another therefore your faults (your slips, your false steps, your** offenses, your sins) and pray [also] for one another, that you may be healed and restored [to a spiritual tone of mind and heart]. The earnest (heartfelt, continued) prayer of a righteous man makes tremendous power available [dynamic in its working] (James 5:16 AMP). We are overcomers by the blood of the Lamb, and by the word of our testimony! (Rev. 12:11.)

Prayer

Father, forgive me for my attempts to hurt and dominate others. I realize that I have released my anger inappropriately. I confess this as sin and receive Your forgiveness, knowing that You are faithful and just to forgive my sin and cleanse me from all unrighteousness. I forgive those who have wronged me, and ask for healing of my anger and unresolved hurts.

I realize that I am responsible for my own behavior, and I am accountable to You for my thoughts, words, and actions.

Thank You for the Holy Spirit Who leads me into reality — the truth that makes me free. You have sent

Your Word and healed me, and delivered me from all my destructions.

Father, I am empowered through my union with You. I draw my strength from You [that strength which Your boundless might provides]. Your strength causes me to be steadfast and trustworthy, gives me the capacity for perseverance and tolerance, and enables me to resist hypersensitivity, irritability, and touchiness.

I desire to be well balanced (temperate, sober of mind), vigilant, and cautious at all times; for I recognize that enemy — the devil — who roams around like a lion roaring, seeking someone to seize upon and devour. In the name of Jesus, I withstand him; firm in faith [against his onset — rooted, established, strong, immovable, and determined].

I am dwelling in the secret place of the Most High, and I shall remain stable and fixed under the shadow of the Almighty [Whose power no foe can withstand].

I purpose to walk in love toward my family members, my associates, and my neighbors with the help of the Holy Spirit. Whom the Son has set free is free indeed.

Thanks be to You, Lord, for You always cause me to triumph in Christ Jesus. I am an overcomer by the blood of the Lamb, and by the word of my testimony.

In Jesus' name, amen.

Scripture References

1 John 1:9	Ephesians 6:10 AMP
Mark 11:24,25	1 Peter 5:8,9 AMP
Matthew 12:36	Psalm 91:1 AMP
John 16:13	John 8:36
John 8:32	2 Corinthians 2:14
Psalm 107:20	Revelation 12:11

Overcoming Chronic Fatigue Syndrome

Introduction

All fatigue does not fall into the category of Chronic Fatigue Syndrome. Most people at one time or another have feelings of apathy and energy loss — times when they go to bed tired and get up tired.

There are cases of fatigue that last for weeks, months, or even years. The medical profession has not determined the causes of Chronic Fatigue Syndrome, and does not know its cure. In most individuals it simply runs its course.[1]

According to those who have shared their experience with this syndrome, they have flu-like symptoms — feel achy with a low-grade fever. One person who suffers from it and for whom we pray is considered disabled and cannot work regularly.

---

[1] Editors of *Prevention* Magazine, *Symptoms, Their Causes & Cures* (Emmaus, PA: Rodale Press, 1994), pp. 179,181.

You and I are created triune beings — spirit, soul, and body. (1 Thess. 5:23.) The Apostle John wrote, **Beloved, I wish above all things that thou mayest prosper and be in health, even as thy soul prospereth** (3 John 2).

God's Word is medicine to our flesh. (Prov. 4:20-22 AMP.) If any type of medication is to bring relief and a cure, it is necessary to follow the prescribed dosage. This is true with "spiritual" medicine. It is imperative to take doses of God's Word daily through reading, meditation, and listening to healing tapes. The spirit, soul, and body are inter-related; it is the Word of God that brings the entire being into harmony.

God made us and knows us inside and out. He sent His Word to heal us and to deliver us from all our destructions. (Ps. 107:20.) Prayer prepares us to take action. Jesus said that if we pray in secret, our heavenly Father will reward us openly. (Matt. 6:6.) Prayer includes praise, worship, and petition.

Prayer prepares us for change — it equips us for action. It puts us in tune and in harmony with the Spirit

Health and Healing

Father, in the name of Jesus, I confess Your Word concerning healing. As I do this, I believe and say that Your Word will not return to You void, but will accomplish what it says it will. Therefore, I believe in the name of Jesus that I am healed, according to 1 Peter 2:24. It is written in Your Word that Jesus himself took our infirmities and bore our sicknesses. Therefore, with great boldness and confidence I say on the authority of that written Word that I am redeemed from the curse of sickness, and I refuse to tolerate its symptoms.

Satan, I speak to you in the name of Jesus and say that your principalities, powers, your spirits who rule the present darkness, and your spiritual wickedness in heavenly places are bound from operating against me in any way. I am the property of Almighty God, and I give you no place in me. I dwell in the secret place of the Most High God. I abide, remain stable and fixed under the shadow of the Almighty, Whose power no foe can withstand.

Now, Father, because I reverence and worship You, I have the assurance of Your Word that the angel of the Lord encamps around about me and delivers me from every evil work. No evil shall befall me, no plague or calamity shall come near my dwelling. I confess the Word of God abides in me and delivers to me perfect soundness of mind and wholeness in body and spirit from the deepest parts of my nature in my immortal spirit even to the joints and marrow of my bones. That Word is medication and life to my flesh for the law of the Spirit of life operates in me and makes me free from the law of sin and death.

I have on the whole armor of God, and the shield of faith protects me from all the fiery darts of the wicked. Jesus is the High Priest of my confession, and I hold fast to my confession of faith in Your Word. I stand immovable and fixed in full assurance that I have health and healing now in the name of Jesus. Amen.

Once this has been prayed, thank the Father that Satan is bound and continue to confess this healing and thank God for it.

Scripture References

Isaiah 55:11	Psalm 91:10
1 Peter 2:24	Psalm 34:7
Matthew 8:17	2 Timothy 1:7
Galatians 3:13	Hebrews 4:12,14
James 4:7	Proverbs 4:22
Ephesians 6:12	Romans 8:2
2 Corinthians 10:4	Ephesians 6:11,16
Psalm 91:1	Psalm 112:7

Safety

Father, in the name of Jesus, I thank You that You watch over Your Word to perform it. I thank You that I dwell in the secret place of the Most High and that I remain stable and fixed under the shadow of the Almighty whose power no foe can withstand.

Father, You are my refuge and my fortress. *No evil shall befall me — no accident shall overtake me — nor any plague or calamity come near my home.* You give Your angels special charge over me, to accompany and defend and preserve me in all my ways of obedience and service. They are encamped around about me.

Father, You are my confidence, firm and strong. You keep my foot from being caught in a trap or hidden danger. Father, You give me safety and ease me — *Jesus is my safety!*

Traveling — As I go, I say, "Let me pass over to the other side," and I have what I say. I walk on my way securely and in confident trust, for my heart and mind

are firmly fixed and stayed on You, and I am kept in
perfect peace.

Sleeping — Father, I sing for joy upon my bed
because You sustain me. In peace I lie down and sleep,
for You alone, Lord, make me dwell in safety. I lie down
and I am not afraid. My sleep is sweet for You give
blessings to me in sleep. Thank You, Father, in Jesus'
name. Amen.

*Continue to feast and meditate upon all of Psalm 91 for
yourself and your loved ones!*

Scripture References

Jeremiah 1:12	Proverbs 3:23 AMP
Psalm 91:1,2 AMP	Psalm 112:7
Psalm 91:10 AMP	Isaiah 26:3
Psalm 91:11 AMP	Psalm 149:5
Psalm 34:7	Psalm 3:5
Proverbs 3:26 AMP	Psalm 4:8 AMP
Isaiah 49:25	Proverbs 3:24
Mark 4:35	Psalm 127:2

Peaceful Sleep

In the name of Jesus, I bind you, Satan, and all your agents from my dreams. I forbid you to interfere in any way with my sleep.

I bring every thought, every imagination, and every dream into the captivity and obedience of Jesus Christ. Father, I thank You that even as I sleep my heart counsels me and reveals to me Your purpose and plan. Thank You for sweet sleep, for You promised Your beloved sweet sleep. Therefore, my heart is glad, and my spirit rejoices. My body and soul rest and confidently dwell in safety. Amen.

Scripture References

Matthew 16:19	Psalm 16:7-9
Matthew 18:18	Psalm 127:2
2 Corinthians 10:5	Proverbs 3:24

Knowing God's Will

Father, in Jesus' name, I thank You that You are instructing me in the way which I should go and that You are guiding me with Your eye. I thank You for Your guidance and leading concerning Your will, Your plan, and Your purpose for my life. I do hear the voice of the Good Shepherd, for I know You and follow You. You lead me in the paths of righteousness for Your name's sake.

Thank You, Father, that my path is growing brighter and brighter until it reaches the full light of day. As I follow You, Lord, I believe my path is becoming clearer each day.

Thank You, Father, that Jesus was made unto me wisdom. Confusion is not a part of my life. I am not confused about Your will for my life. I trust in You and lean not unto my own understanding. As I acknowledge You in all my ways, You are directing my paths. I believe that as I trust in You completely, You will show me the path of life. Amen.

Scripture References

Psalm 32:8	1 Corinthians 1:30
John 10:3,4	1 Corinthians 14:33
Psalm 23:3	Proverbs 3:5,6
Proverbs 4:18	Psalm 16:11
Ephesians 5:19	

Godly Wisdom in the Affairs of Life

Father, You said if anyone lacks wisdom, let him ask of You, Who giveth to all men liberally, and upbraideth not; and it shall be given him. Therefore, I ask in faith, nothing wavering, to be filled with the knowledge of Your will in all wisdom and spiritual understanding. Today I incline my ear unto wisdom, and apply my heart to understanding so that I might receive that which has been freely given unto me.

In the name of Jesus, I receive skill and godly wisdom and instruction. I discern and comprehend the words of understanding and insight. I receive instruction in wise dealing and the discipline of wise thoughtfulness, righteousness, justice, and integrity. Prudence, knowledge, discretion, and discernment are given to me. I increase in knowledge. As a person of understanding, I acquire skill and attain to sound counsels [so that I may be able to steer my course rightly].

Wisdom will keep, defend, and protect me; I love her and she guards me. I prize Wisdom highly and exalt her; she will bring me to honor because I embrace her. She gives to my head a wreath of gracefulness; a crown of beauty and glory will she deliver to me. Length of days is in her right hand, and in her left hand are riches and honor.

Jesus has been made unto me wisdom, and in Him are all the treasures of [divine] wisdom, [of comprehensive insight into the ways and purposes of God], and [all the riches of spiritual] knowledge and enlightenment are stored up and lie hidden. God has hidden away sound and godly wisdom and stored it up for me, for I am the righteousness of God in Christ Jesus.

Therefore, I will walk in paths of uprightness. When I walk, my steps shall not be hampered — my path will be clear and open; and when I run I shall not stumble. I take fast hold of instruction, and do not let her go; I guard her, for she is my life. I let my eyes look right on [with fixed purpose], and my gaze is straight before me. I consider well the path of my feet, and I let all my ways be established and ordered aright.

Father, in the name of Jesus, I look carefully to how I walk! I live purposefully and worthily and accurately, not as unwise and witless, but as a wise — sensible, intelligent person; making the very most of my time — buying up every opportunity. Amen.

Scripture References

James 1:5,6a	1 Corinthians 1:30
Colossians 1:9b	Colossians 2:3 AMP
Proverbs 2:2	Proverbs 2:7 AMP
Proverbs 1:2-5 AMP	2 Corinthians 5:21
Proverbs 4:6,8,9 AMP	Proverbs 4:11-13,25,26 AMP
Proverbs 3:16 AMP	Ephesians 5:15,16 AMP

Receiving a Discerning Heart

Father, I thank You for creating within me a wise and discerning heart, so that I am able to distinguish between right and wrong.

This is my prayer: that my love may abound more and more in knowledge and depth of insight, so that I may be able to discern what is best and may be pure and blameless until the day of Christ, filled with the fruit of righteousness that comes through Jesus Christ — to Your glory and praise, O Lord.

Father, I trust in You with all my heart and lean not on my own understanding; in all my ways I acknowledge You, and You will make my paths straight. Through Your precepts I get understanding; therefore I hate every false way. Your Word is a lamp to my feet, and a light to my path.

Joseph in Genesis 41:39-41 NIV was described as a discerning and wise man who was put in charge of the entire land of Egypt. As You were with Joseph, so shall You be with me. You will cause me to find favor at my place of employment, at home, or wherever I may be.

Boldness

Father, in the name of Jesus, I am of good courage, I pray that You grant to me that with all *boldness* I speak forth Your Word. I pray that freedom of utterance be given me that I may open my mouth to proclaim *boldly* the mystery of the good news of the Gospel — that I may declare it *boldly* as I ought to do.

Father, I believe I receive that *boldness* now in the name of Jesus. Therefore, I have *boldness* to enter into the Holy of Holies by the blood of Jesus. Because of my faith in Him, I dare to have the *boldness* (courage and confidence) of free access — an unreserved approach to You with freedom and without fear. I can draw fearlessly and confidently and *boldly* near to Your throne of grace and receive mercy and find grace to help in good time for my every need. I am *bold* to pray. I come to the throne of God with my petitions, and for others who do not know how to ascend to the throne.

I will be *bold* toward Satan, demons, evil spirits, sickness, disease, and poverty for Jesus is the Head of all rule and authority — of every angelic principality and power. Disarming those who were ranged against us, Jesus made a *bold* display and public example of them triumphing over them. I am *bold* to say, "Satan, you are a defeated foe, for my God and my Jesus reign!"

I take comfort and am encouraged and confidently and *boldly* say, "The Lord is my Helper, I will not be seized with alarm — I will not fear or dread or be terrified. What can man do to me?" I dare to proclaim the Word toward heaven, toward hell, and toward earth. I am *bold* as a lion for I have been made the righteousness of God in Christ Jesus. I am complete in Him! Praise the name of Jesus! Amen.

Scripture References

Psalm 27:14	Hebrews 4:16 AMP
Acts 4:29	Colossians 2:10,15 AMP
Ephesians 6:19,20 AMP	Hebrews 13:6 AMP
Mark 11:23,24	Proverbs 28:1
Hebrews 10:19 AMP, KJV	2 Corinthians 5:21
Ephesians 3:12 AMP	

Being Equipped for Success

Father, I thank You that the entrance of Your words gives light. I thank You that Your Word which You speak *(and which I speak)* is alive and full of power —making it active, operative, energizing, and effective. I thank You, Father, that [You have given me a spirit] of power, and of love, and of a calm and well-balanced mind, and discipline, and self-control. I have Your power and ability and sufficiency, for You have qualified me (making me to be fit and worthy and sufficient) as a minister and dispenser of a new covenant [of salvation through Christ].

In the name of Jesus, I walk out of the realm of failure into the arena of success, giving thanks to You, Father, for You have qualified and made me fit to share the portion which is the inheritance of the saints (God's holy people) in the Light.

Father, You have delivered and drawn me to Yourself out of the control and the dominion of darkness *(failure, doubt and fear)* and have transferred me into the Kingdom of the Son of Your love, in Whom there is good success [and freedom from fears, agitating passions, and moral conflicts]. I rejoice in Jesus Who has come that I might have life and have it more abundantly.

Today I am a new creation, for I am (ingrafted) in Christ, the Messiah. The old (previous moral and spiritual condition) has passed away. Behold, the fresh and new has come! I forget those things which are behind me and reach forth unto those things which are before me. I am crucified with Christ: nevertheless I live; yet not I, but Christ lives in me: and the life which I now live in the flesh I live by the faith of the Son of God, Who loved me, and gave Himself for me.

Today I attend to the Word of God. I consent and submit to Your sayings, Father. Your words shall not depart from my sight; I will keep them in the midst of my heart. For they are life [success] to me, healing and health to all my flesh. I keep my heart with all vigilance and above all that I guard, for out of it flow the springs of life.

Today I will not let mercy and kindness and truth forsake me. I bind them about my neck; I write them upon the tablet of my heart. So therefore I will find favor, good understanding, and high esteem in the sight [or judgment] of God and man.

Today my delight and desire are in the law of the Lord, and on His law I habitually meditate (ponder and study) by day and by night. Therefore I am like a tree firmly planted [and tended] by the streams of water, ready to bring forth my fruit in my season; my leaf also shall not fade or wither, and everything I do shall prosper [and come to maturity].

Now thanks be to God, Who always causes me to triumph in Christ!

In His name I pray, amen.

Scripture References

Psalm 119:130	Philippians 3:13b
Hebrews 4:12a AMP	Galatians 2:20
2 Timothy 1:7b AMP	Proverbs 4:20-23 AMP
2 Corinthians 3:5b-6a AMP	Proverbs 3:3,4 AMP
Colossians 1:12,13 AMP	Psalm 1:2,3 AMP
2 Corinthians 5:17 AMP	2 Corinthians 2:14
John 10:10b	

Prayer for the Success of a Business

Father, Your Word says that I am a partaker of the inheritance and treasures of heaven. You have delivered me out of the authority of darkness and translated me into the kingdom of Your dear Son. Father, where Your Word is there is light and, also, understanding. Your Word does not return to You void but always accomplishes what it is sent to do. I am a joint-heir with Jesus and as Your son/daughter, I accept that the communication of my faith is effectual by the acknowledging of every good work which is in me in Christ Jesus.

Father, I commit my works (the plans and cares of my business) to You, entrust them wholly to You. Since You are effectually at work in me, You cause my thoughts to become agreeable with Your will, so that my business plans shall be established and succeed. In the name of Jesus, I submit to every kind of wisdom, practical insight and prudence which You have lavished upon me in accordance with the riches and generosity of Your gracious favor.

Father, I affirm that I obey Your Word by making an honest living with my own hands so that I may be able to give to those in need. In Your strength and according to Your grace I provide for myself and my own family. Thank You, Father, for making all grace, every favor and earthly blessing come to me in abundance that I, having all sufficiency, may abound to every good work.

Father, thank You for the ministering spirits that You have assigned to go forth to bring in consumers. Jesus said, "You are the light of the world." In His Name my light shall so shine before all men that they may see my good works glorifying You, my heavenly Father.

Thank You for the grace to remain diligent in seeking knowledge and skill in areas where I am inexperienced. I ask You for wisdom and the ability to understand righteousness, justice, and fair dealing in every area and relationship. I affirm that I am faithful and committed to Your Word. My life and business are founded upon its principles.

Father, thank You for the success of my business!

In Your name, amen.

Scripture References

Romans 8:17	1 Timothy 5:8
Colossians 1:12	2 Corinthians 9:8
Psalm 119:130	Hebrews 1:14
Philemon 1:6	Matthew 5:14,16
Proverbs 16:3	Proverbs 22:29
Philippians 2:13	Proverbs 2:9
Ephesians 1:7,8	Proverbs 4:20-22
Ephesians 4:28	

The Setting of Proper Priorities

Father, in the name of Jesus, I come before You. Spirit of Truth, Who comes from the Father, it is You Who guides me into all truth. According to 3 John 2 it is God's will that I prosper in every way and that my body keeps well, even as my soul keeps well and prospers.

One thing I ask of You, Lord, one thing will I seek after, inquire for and [insistently] require, that I may dwell in Your house [in Your presence], all the days of my life, to behold and gaze upon Your beauty. I come to meditate, consider and inquire in Your temple *(about success in life)*.

Father, You have said, **I will not in any way fail you nor give you up nor leave you without support. [I will] not, [I will] not, [I will] not in any degree leave you helpless, nor forsake nor let [you] down, [relax my hold on you]. — Assuredly not!** (Heb. 13:5 AMP). So I take comfort and am encouraged and confidently and boldly say that the Lord is my Helper, I will not be seized with alarm — I will not fear or dread or be terrified. What can man do to me?

In the name of Jesus, I am strong and very courageous, that I may do according to all Your Word. I turn not from it to the right hand or to the left, that I may prosper wherever I go. The Word of God shall not depart out of my mouth, but I shall meditate on it day and night. I hear therefore and am watchful to keep the instructions, the laws and precepts of my Lord God, that it may be well with me and that I may increase exceedingly, as the Lord God has promised me, in a land flowing with milk and honey. The Lord my God is one Lord — the only Lord. And I shall love the Lord my God with all my [mind and] heart, and with my entire being, and with all my might. And I will love my neighbor as myself.

Jesus, You said that when I do this I will live — enjoy active, blessed, endless life in the Kingdom of God. Therefore, I will not worry or be anxious about what I am going to eat, or what I am going to have to drink, or what I am going to have to wear. My heavenly

Father knows that I need them all. But I purpose in my heart to seek for (aim at and strive after) first of all Your Kingdom, Lord, and Your righteousness [Your way of doing and being right], and then all these things taken together will be given me besides.

Now thanks be to You, Father, Who always causes me to triumph in Christ! Amen.

Scripture References

John 16:13a	Deuteronomy 6:1,3-5 AMP
Psalm 27:4 AMP	Luke 10:27,28 AMP
Hebrews 13:5b,6 AMP	Matthew 6:31-33 AMP
Joshua 1:7,8a AMP	2 Corinthians 2:14

Maintaining Good Relations

Father, in the name of Jesus, I will not withhold good from those to whom it is due [its rightful owners], when it is in the power of my hand to do it. I will render to all men their dues. I will [pay] taxes to whom taxes are due, revenue to whom revenue is due, respect to whom respect is due, and honor to whom honor is due.

I will not lose heart and grow weary and faint in acting nobly and doing nobly and right, for in due season I shall reap, if I do not loosen and relax my courage and faint. So then, as occasion and opportunity open up to me, I will do good [morally] to all people [not only being useful or profitable to them, but also doing what is for their spiritual good and advantage]. I am mindful to be a blessing, especially to those of the household of faith [those who belong to God's family with me, the believers].

I will not contend with a man for no reason — when he has done me no wrong. If possible, as far as it depends on me, I purpose to live at peace with everyone. Amen.

Scripture References

Proverbs 3:27 AMP   Proverbs 3:30 AMP

Romans 13:7 AMP   Romans 12:18 AMP

Galatians 6:9,10 AMP

Improving Communication Skills

Introduction

Lack of communication skills is one of the greatest hindrances to healthy relationships. Most of the time, when we pray, we are seeking change. We cannot change others, but we can submit to the constant ministry of transformation by the Holy Spirit. (Rom. 12:1,2.)

Prayer prepares us for change. Change produces change, which may be uncomfortable. If we will move through the discomfort, God will work with us, leading us out of our self-developed defense mechanisms into a place of victory. In this place He heals our brokenness, becomes our defense and our vindication. We are enabled to submit to the Champion of our salvation, which we are working out with fear and trembling. (Phil. 2:12.)

Adults who grew up in judgmental, critical homes where they were never allowed to express themselves sometimes carry much hurt and anger into their relationships. Often, they were not permitted to have their own feelings without being condemned; they were not permitted to explore any ideas different from their parents or caregivers. There was an eye watching their every move. Any punishment they received was justified. Their parents were incapable of making a mistake.

Adult children of religiously rigid environments were led to believe that any slip, error in judgment, or mistake was a sin that would send them straight to hell; the parent's religious doctrine was the only way to heaven; and to deviate from it would lead to destruction. Forgiveness could be attained only after much sorrow, penance, and retribution. Death before the completion of repentance led to an eternity in hell.

People raised in such oppressive home environments were never allowed to find themselves or to travel their own individual spiritual journeys leading to truth. Their parents, especially the father-figure in the home, was God in the flesh. Conflict resolution was never taught or practiced. Whatever the head of the household said was law — and disobedience to his law was not discussed, but beaten out of the child. The wife was subservient and was not allowed to question the dictates of the husband.

When these adults marry, they often feel that they have finally found a platform from which to express themselves. They have escaped a place of abiding fear, constant condemnation, and continual criticism. Having no communication skills, they often have difficulty expressing themselves properly. When anyone disagrees with them, they tend to react as they were taught. Only now, the marriage partner or friend does not submit to dogmatic, manipulative words. Frustration develops. The adult child seeks to make himself or herself understood, resulting in more frustration. Anger is fed, and the individual continues to be in bondage to the idea that he or she should never have been born. The person either retreats to a silent corner, refusing to talk, or uses words to build walls of defense — shutting others out. He or she resides inside emotional isolation, attempting to remove himself or herself from more hurt and criticism.

There is a way of escape. God sent His Word to heal us and to deliver us from all our destructions. (Ps.

107:20.) We must determine to listen, to learn, and to change with the help of the Holy Spirit — our Teacher, our Guide, and our Intercessor. The anointing is upon Jesus to bind up and heal our emotional wounds. (Luke 4:18.) His anointing destroys every yoke of bondage (Is. 10:27), setting the captives free.

Prayer

Father, I am Your child. Jesus said that if I pray to You in secret, You will reward me openly.

Father, I desire with all my heart to walk in love, but I am ever sabotaging my own efforts and failing in my relationships. I know that without faith it is impossible to please and be satisfactory to You. I am coming near to You, believing that You exist and that You are the rewarder of those who earnestly and diligently seek You.

Show "me" to me. Uncover — bring everything to the light — when anything is exposed and reproved by the light, it is made visible and clear; and where everything is visible and clear there is light.

Heal the past wounds and hurts which have controlled my behavior and my speech. Teach me to guard my heart with all diligence, for out of it flow the very issues of life. Teach me to speak the truth in love in my home, in my church, with my friends and in all my relationships. Also, help me to realize that others have a right to express themselves. Help me to make room for their ideas, their opinions, even when they are different from mine.

Words are powerful. The power of life and death is in the tongue, and You said that I would eat the fruit of it.

Father, I realize that words can be creative or destructive. A word out of my mouth may seem of no account, but it can accomplish nearly anything — or destroy it! A careless or wrongly placed word out of my mouth can set off a forest fire. By my speech I can ruin the world, turn harmony to chaos, throw mud on a reputation, send the whole world up in smoke, and go up in smoke with it, smoke right from the pit of hell. This is scary!

Father, forgive me for speaking curses and blessings. I am reacting out of past hurts and unresolved anger. At times I am dogmatic, even boasting that I am wise; sometimes, unknowingly I have twisted the truth to make myself sound wise; at times I have tried to look better than others, or get the better of another; my words have contributed to things falling apart. My human anger is misdirected and works unrighteousness.

Father, forgive me. I cannot change myself, but I am willing to change and walk in the wisdom that is from above.

Father, I submit to that wisdom from above that begins with a holy life and is characterized by getting along with others. It is gentle and reasonable, overflowing with mercy and blessings, not hot one day and cold the next, not two-faced. Use me as Your instrument to develop a healthy, robust community that lives right with You. I will enjoy its results only if I do the hard work of getting along with others, treating them with dignity and honor.

With the help of the Holy Spirit and by Your grace, I will not let any unwholesome talk come out of my mouth, but only what is helpful for building others up according to their needs, that it may benefit those who listen.

My heart overflows with a goodly theme; I address my psalm to You, the King. My tongue is like the pen of a ready writer. Mercy and kindness shut out all hatred and selfishness, and truth shuts out all deliberate hypocrisy or falsehood; and I bind them about my neck, write them upon the tablet of my heart.

I speak excellent and princely things; and the opening of my lips shall be for right things. My mouth shall utter truth, and wrongdoing is detestable and loathsome to my lips. All the words of my mouth are righteous (upright and in right standing with You, Lord); there is nothing contrary to truth or crooked in them. My tongue is as choice silver, and my lips feed and guide many. I open my mouth in skillful and godly wisdom, and on my tongue is the law of kindness [giving counsel and instruction].

Father, thank You for loving me unconditionally. I thank You for sending Your Son Jesus to be my Friend and elder Brother and for giving me Your Holy Spirit to teach me and to bring all things to my remembrance. I am an overcomer by the blood of the Lamb, and by the word of my testimony.

In the name of Jesus I pray, amen.

Scripture References

1 John 3:1	Ephesians 4:29 NIV
Matthew 6:6	Psalm 45:1 AMP
Hebrews 11:6 AMP	Proverbs 3:3 AMP
Ephesians 5:13 AMP	Proverbs 8:6-8 AMP
Proverbs 4:23	Proverbs 10:20,21 AMP
Ephesians 4:15	Proverbs 31:26 AMP
Proverbs 18:21	Romans 8:31-39 NIV
James 3:5,6 MESSAGE	Hebrews 2:11 NIV
James 3:9-16 MESSAGE	John 15:15 NIV
James 3:17	John 14:26
James 3:17,18 MESSAGE	Revelation 12:11

Prosperity

Father, in the name of Your Son, Jesus, I confess Your Word over my finances this day. As I do this, I say it with my mouth and believe it in my heart and know that Your Word will not return to You void, but will accomplish what it says it will do.

Therefore, I believe in the name of Jesus that all my needs are met, according to Philippians 4:19. I believe that because I have given tithes and offerings to further your cause, Father, gifts will be given to me, good measure, pressed down, shaken together, and running over will they pour into my bosom. For with the measure I deal out, it will be measured back to me.

Father, You have delivered me out of the authority of darkness into the Kingdom of Your dear Son. Father, I have taken my place as your child. I thank You that You have assumed Your place as my Father and have made Your home with me. You are taking care of me and even now are enabling me to walk in love and in wisdom, and to walk in the fullness of fellowship with Your Son.

Satan, I bind you from my finances, according to Matthew 18:18, and loose you from your assignment against me, in the name of Jesus.

Father, I thank You that Your ministering spirits are now free to minister for me and bring in the necessary finances.

Father, I confess You are a very present help in trouble, and You are more than enough. I confess, God You are able to make all grace — every favor and earthly blessing — come to me in abundance, so that I am always, and in all circumstances furnished in abundance for every good work and charitable donation. Amen.

Scripture References

Isaiah 55:11	2 Corinthians 6:16,18
Philippians 4:19	Matthew 18:18
Luke 6:38	Hebrews 1:14
Mark 10:29,30	2 Corinthians 9:8 AMP
Colossians 1:13	Psalm 46:1

Dedication for Your Tithes

I profess this day unto the Lord God that I have come into the inheritance which the Lord swore to give me. I am in the land which You have provided for me in Jesus Christ, the Kingdom of Almighty God. I was a sinner serving Satan; he was my god. But I called upon the name of Jesus, and You heard my cry and delivered me into the Kingdom of Your dear Son.

Jesus, as my Lord and High Priest, I bring the first fruits of my income to You and worship the Lord my God with it.

I rejoice in all the good which You have given to me and my household. I have hearkened to the voice of the Lord my God and have done according to all that He has commanded me. Now look down from your holy habitation from heaven and bless me as You said in Your Word. I thank You, Father, in Jesus' name. Amen.

Scripture References

Deuteronomy 26:1,3,
  10,11,14,15 AMP

Ephesians 2:1-5

Colossians 1:13

Hebrews 3:1,7,8

Selling Real Estate

Father, I thank You for the skillful and godly wisdom needed in offering my house (or other real estate) to be sold. I am preparing my house (property) in excellence that it may be beautiful and desirable as though I am preparing it for Your habitation. I am asking a fair and competitive market price, and will not take advantage of a potential buyer.

Father, I ask that You prepare and send a ready, willing, and able buyer to purchase my house (property). A person who has the funds available to pay the fair market value, pre-qualified and approved by a lending institution. One who has perfect timing of possession that fits into my need and his/hers.

Thank You for going before me and preparing the way. In the name of Jesus, I seek and pursue peace, thanking You that the spirit of truth shall prevail in our deliberations. I declare and decree that everyone involved speaks truly, deals truly, and lives truly.

Should there be anything that is hidden, I ask that it be revealed and brought to the light. Truth and mercy are written upon the tablets of my heart, and I have favor, good understanding, and high esteem in Your sight and in the sight of the potential buyer.

In the name of Jesus, amen.

Scripture References

Proverbs 2:6,9,12,15 AMP   1 Corinthians 4:5 AMP

1 Corinthians 2:9   Proverbs 3:3,4 AMP

Ephesians 4:15 AMP

In Court Cases

Father, in the name of Jesus, it is written in Your Word to call on You and You will answer me and show me great and mighty things. I put You in remembrance of Your Word and thank You that You watch over it to perform it.

I say that no weapon formed against me shall prosper and any tongue that rises against me in judgment I shall show to be in the wrong. This peace, security, and triumph over opposition is my inheritance as Your child. This is the righteousness which I obtain from You, Father, which You impart to me as my justification. I am far from even the thought of destruction, for I shall not fear and terror shall not come near me.

Father, You say You will establish me to the end — keep me steadfast, give me strength, and guarantee my vindication; that is, be my warrant against all accusation or indictment. Father, You contend with those who contend with me, and You perfect that which concerns me. I dwell in the secret place of the Most High, and this secret place hides me from the strife of tongues, for a false witness who breathes out lies is an abomination to You.

I am a true witness and all my words are upright and in right standing with You, Father. By my long forbearing and calmness of spirit the judge is persuaded, and my soft speech breaks down the most bonelike resistance. Therefore, I am not anxious beforehand how I shall reply in defense or what I am to say, for the Holy Spirit teaches me *in that very hour* and moment what I ought to say to those in the outside world. My speech is seasoned with salt.

I thank You, Father, that Satan and all menacing spirits are bound from operating against me, for I am strong in You, Lord, and in the power of Your might. Your shield of faith quenches every fiery dart. Thank You, Father, that I increase in wisdom and in stature and years, and in favor with You, God, and man. Praise the Lord! Amen.

Scripture References

Jeremiah 33:3   Proverbs 6:19

Jeremiah 1:12 AMP   Proverbs 14:25

Isaiah 43:26 AMP   Proverbs 8:8 AMP

Isaiah 54:17 AMP   Proverbs 25:15 AMP

Isaiah 54:14 AMP   Luke 12:11,12 AMP

1 Corinthians 1:8 AMP   Colossians 4:6

Isaiah 49:25   Matthew 18:18

Psalm 138:8   Ephesians 6:10,16

Psalm 91:1   Luke 2:52 AMP

Psalm 31:20

Protection for Travel

Father, today, in Jesus' name, I confess Your Word over my travel plans and know that Your Word does not go out and return to You void, but it accomplishes what You say it will do. I give You thanks for moving quickly to perform Your Word and fulfill its promises.

As I prepare to travel, I rejoice in the promises that Your Word holds for protection and safety of the righteous. Only You, Father, make me live in safety. I trust in You and dwell in Your protection. If I shall face any problems or trouble, I will run to You, Father, my strong tower and shelter in time of need. Believing in the written Word of God, I speak peace, safety and success over my travel plans, in Jesus' name.

As a child of God, my path of travel is preserved and angels keep charge over me and surround my car/airplane/ship. I will proceed with my travel plans without fear of accidents, problems or any type of frustrations. I have the peace of God and will allow fear no place as I travel; the Lord delivers me from every type of evil and preserves me for His kingdom. I stand confident that my travel plans will not be disrupted or confused.

Thank You, Father, that in every situation You are there to protect me. No matter in what means of transportation I choose to travel, You have redeemed me and will protect me. The earth and all things on it are under Your command. You are my Heavenly Father. Through my faith in You, I have the power to tread on serpents and have all power over the enemy. No food or water will harm me when I arrive at my destination. My travel is safe.

Father, I give You the glory in this situation. Thank You that as I keep Your ways before me, I will be safe. Your mercy is upon me and my family, and our travels will be safe. Not a hair on our heads shall perish. Thank You, Father, for Your guidance and safety — You are worthy of all praise! Amen.

Scripture References

Isaiah 55:11   Isaiah 43:1-3

The Scriptures condemn pre-marital sex, fornication, adultery, and all forms of sexual perversion. (Matt. 15:19; Mark 7:21 AMP; Gal. 5:19-21; Col. 3:5,6.) Although sexual desires are not a sin, if not properly controlled, those desires can lead to sin.

According to James 1:13-15, sin begins with a thought conceived from lust. Lust is not limited to sex. It is possible to lust after many things that can cause sin. That's why it is so important to take control over the mind and heart to keep them pure and holy — in spite of temptation.

One of the myths that has ensnared many single people is the mistaken idea that marriage will automatically release them from the temptation to sin. Without repentance and the renewing of the mind, those who have a problem with lustful thoughts before they are married will have the same problem after they are married, just as those who have a problem with sexual perversion before marriage will continue to have the same problem after marriage.

One married man shared his testimony of deliverance from pornography. He was having to continually guard himself from mental images that kept reappearing.

Marriage is not a cure-all for sexual sins or any other sin.

Yes, God does understand. With every temptation He has provided a way of escape. (1 Cor. 10:13.)

Yes, there is forgiveness for sin (1 John 1:9) — through God's abounding grace. (Rom. 5:20.) The question is: **...Are we to remain in sin in order that God's grace (favor and mercy) may multiply and overflow? Certainly not! How can we who died to sin live in it any longer?** (Rom. 6:1,2 AMP.)

We who are in Christ desire to bring glory to the Father. We cannot do so in our own strength. It is remaining, abiding in union with Jesus that ensures answered prayer, of loving as Jesus loves. (John 15:7-9.) If our prayers are not being answered, it is time to check our love walk. We must ask ourselves, "Are we keeping ourselves in the love of God — remaining vitally united with Jesus?"

> We know [absolutely] that anyone born of
> God does not [deliberately and knowingly] prac-
> tice committing sin, but the One Who was
> begotten of God carefully watches over and
> protects him [Christ's divine presence within
> him preserves him against the evil], and the
> wicked one does not lay hold (get a grip) on him
> or touch [him].

> 1 John 5:18 AMP

This verse says that the wicked one cannot touch us. What is the condition? Having Christ's presence within, staying united with Him — abiding in Him and allowing His Word to abide in us.

If you want to abide in Christ and have His Word abide in you, pray the following prayer with a sincere and believing heart.

Prayer

Lord, I am abiding in Your Word [holding fast to Your teachings and living in accordance with them]. It is my desire to be Your true disciple. I am abiding in (vitally united to) the vine. I cannot bear fruit unless I abide in You.

Lord, because You are the Vine, and I am a branch living in You, I bear much (abundant) fruit. Apart from You [cut off from vital union with You] I can do nothing. Your Son Jesus said, **If you live in Me [abide vitally united to Me] and My words remain in you and continue to live in your hearts, ask whatever you will, and it shall be done for you** (John 15:7 AMP).

When I bear (produce) much fruit, You Father, are honored and glorified. By Your grace that I have received, I will show and prove myself to be a true follower of Your Son Jesus. He has loved me, [just] as You, Father, have loved Him. I am abiding in that love.

Lord, You have assured me that if I keep Your commandments [if I continue to obey Your instructions], I will abide in Your love and live on in it, just as Your Son Jesus obeyed Your commandments and lived on in Your love. He told me these things, that Your joy and delight may be in me, and that my joy and gladness may be of full measure and complete and overflowing. This is Your commandment; that we love one another [just] as You have loved us.

Father, thank You for Your Word — it is the truth that makes me free. I am born (begotten) of You, Lord, and I do not [deliberately, knowingly, and habitually] practice sin. Your nature abides in me [Your principle of life, the divine sperm, remains permanently within me]; and I cannot practice sinning because I am born (begotten) of You. I have hidden Your Word in my heart that I might not sin against You.

May Christ through my faith [actually] dwell (settle down, abide, make His permanent home) in my heart! It is my desire to be rooted deep in love and founded securely on love, that I may have the power and be strong to apprehend and grasp with all the saints [Your devoted people, the experience of that love] what is the breadth and length and height and depth [of it].

I pray, in the name of Jesus, that I may know this love that surpasses knowledge — that I may be filled to the measure of all Your fullness. Now to You Who are able to do immeasurably more than all I ask or imagine, according to Your power that is at work within me, to You be glory in the Church and in Christ Jesus throughout all generations, forever and ever! Amen.

Scripture References

John 8:31 AMP	1 John 3:9 AMP
John 15:4,5 AMP	Psalm 119:11
John 15:7-12 AMP	Ephesians 3:17,18 AMP
John 8:32	Ephesians 3:19-21 NIV
John 17:17	

Knowing God's Plan for Marriage

Unto You, O Lord, do I bring my life. O my God, I trust in, lean on, rely on, and am confident in You. Let me not be put to shame or [my hope in You] be disappointed; let not my enemies (rejection, hurt, inferiority, unworthiness) triumph over me.

Father, it is written, **For I know the thoughts and plans that I have for you, says the Lord, thoughts and plans for welfare and peace and not for evil, to give you hope in your final outcome. Then you will call upon Me, and you will come and pray to Me, and I will hear and heed you. Then you will seek Me, inquire for, and require Me [as a vital necessity] and find Me when you search for Me with all your heart. I will be found by you, says the Lord...** (Jer. 29:11-14 AMP).

In the name of Jesus, I always pray and do not turn coward (faint, lose heart, and give up).

Father, I am looking for Your plan, Your answer for my life. It is my desire to be married. But, I must be sure in my decision that I am living as You intend and accepting whatever situation You have put me into. According to Your Word, marriage will bring extra problems that I may not need to face at this time in my life.

All the ways of a man or woman are pure in his or her own eyes, but You, Lord weigh the spirits (the thoughts and intents of the heart). Therefore, I roll my works upon You, [commit and trust them wholly to You; You will cause my thoughts to become agreeable to Your will, and] so shall my plans be established and succeed.

Because You, Lord, are my Shepherd, I have everything I need!

You let me rest in the meadow grass and lead me beside the quiet streams. You give me new strength. You help me do what honors You the most.

Even when walking through the dark valley of death I will not be afraid, for You are close beside me, guarding, guiding me all the way.

You provide delicious food for me in the presence of my enemies. You have welcomed me as Your guest; my blessings overflow!

Your goodness and unfailing kindness shall be with me all of my life, and afterwards I will live with You forever in Your home.

In Jesus' name I pray, amen.

Scripture References

Psalm 25:1,2 AMP   Proverbs 16:2,3 AMP

Luke 18:1 AMP   Psalm 23:1-6 TLB

1 Corinthians 7:1,2 TLB

Finding a Mate

Introduction

In our ministry we hear from many men and women who desire to be married. If that is your desire, we encourage you to ask the Lord to prepare you for marriage. Submit to God's future plans for your life, and purpose to please Him. Do not make your deliberations, without knowing His will, at the expense of your personal spiritual growth and transformation. Going from glory to glory (2 Cor. 3:18) is not dependent on having a spouse.

Most of the time, each partner brings a lot of emotional baggage into the marriage relationship. As you prepare for marriage, remember that the anointing that was upon Jesus (Luke 4:18,19) is within you. This anointing will destroy every yoke of bondage (Is. 10:27) as God exposes emotional wounds and heals your brokenness.

Knowing the reality of your completeness in Christ Jesus will enable you to enter into a healthy relationship, one in which both you and your partner will grow

teachers, preachers, counselors — and to things —
books, tapes, seminars — anyone and anything You can
use to teach me Your ways of being and doing right and
being whole.

Teach me how to choose the mate You would have
for me. Give me the wisdom I need to see clearly, and
not to be double-minded. Help me to recognize the
qualities You would have me look for in a mate.

Father, thank You for revealing to me that the
choice of a mate is not to be based only on emotions
and feelings, but that You have very definite guidelines
in the Bible for me to use. I know that when I put these
principles into practice, I will save myself a lot of pain
and trouble.

Thank You that You are not trying to make things
hard for me, but that You know me better than I know
myself. You know my situation — You know the beginning from the end. You know the qualities and attrib-
utes that are needed in another person that will make
me happy in our shared life together and that person
happy with me.

I pray that you will keep my foot from being caught in a hidden trap of danger. I cast the care of this decision on You, knowing that You will cause my thoughts to come in line with Your will so that my plans will be established and succeed.

In Jesus' name I pray, amen.

Scripture References

1 Corinthians 1:3,4 NIV James 1:5-8

Ephesians 4:15   Proverbs 3:26 AMP

Matthew 6:33 AMP   Proverbs 16:3 AMP

Committing to a Life of Purity

Father, I come before Your throne of grace in the name of Jesus. At one time I walked [habitually], following the course and fashion of this world [under the sway of the tendency of this present age]. I lived and conducted myself in the passions of my flesh [my behavior governed by my corrupt and sensual nature], obeying the impulses of the flesh, and the thoughts of my mind [my cravings dictated by my senses and my dark imaginings].

But God — You are so rich in Your mercy! Even when I was dead (slain) by [my own] shortcomings and trespasses, You made me alive together in union with Christ, and it is by Your grace (Your favor and mercy that I did not deserve) that I am saved (delivered from judgment and made a partaker of Christ's salvation). You raised me up together with Him and made us sit down together [giving me joint seating with Him] in the heavenly sphere in Christ Jesus (the Messiah, the Anointed One).

You are my Father, I am Your child. Since I am in Christ, I am a new creature; old things have passed away; and, behold, all things have become new.

In accordance with Your Word, I rid myself of all malice and all deceit, hypocrisy, envy, and slander of every kind. Like a newborn baby, I crave pure spiritual milk, so that by it I may grow up in my salvation, now that I have tasted that You, Lord, are good.

Father, forgive me for the years of watching, reading, and listening to vile things. I submit to Jesus Christ Who loves me and gave Himself up for me, so that He might sanctify me, having cleansed me by the washing of water with the Word, that He might present me to Himself in glorious splendor, without spot or wrinkle or any such things [that I might be holy and faultless].

Thank You for the blood of Christ, Who through the eternal Spirit offered Himself unblemished to You, which cleanses my conscience from acts that lead to death, so that I may serve You, the living God! Thank You for the Holy Spirit Who indwells me. He is holy (chaste, pure).

I ask for and receive an impartation of the wisdom that comes from heaven — it is first of all pure; then peace-loving, considerate, submissive, full of mercy and good fruit, impartial, and sincere.

May my words issue from a pure heart, and may they be pleasing to You.

Lord, Your Holy Spirit is my Counselor — [change my impure language] and give to me a clear and pure speech from pure lips, that I may call upon Your name, to serve You.

I am transformed (changed) by the [entire] renewal of my mind, and I bring my thoughts into obedience to Your Word. I fix my thoughts on what is true and good and right. I determine to think about things that are pure and lovely, and dwell on the fine, good things in others. I think about all I can praise You for, and I am glad. I keep and guard my heart with all vigilance and above all that I guard, for out of it flow the springs of life.

What [an incredible] quality of love You have given (shown, bestowed upon) me, that I should [be permitted to] be named and called and counted a child of God! I am [even here and] now Your child; it is not yet disclosed (made clear) what I shall be [hereafter], but I know that when Jesus comes and is manifested, I shall [as Your child] resemble and be like Him, for I shall see Him just as He [really] is. I have this hope [resting] on Him, and I cleanse (purify) myself just as He is pure (chaste, undefiled, guiltless).

Through the power of the Holy Spirit given to me, I am an overcomer by the blood of the Lamb, and by the word of my testimony!

In Jesus' name I pray, amen.

Scripture References

Ephesians 2:2-6 AMP	Proverbs 15:16 AMP
2 Corinthians 5:17	Zephaniah 3:9 AMP
1 Peter 2:1,2 NIV	Romans 12:2 AMP
Psalm 101:3 NIV	2 Corinthians 10:5
Ephesians 5:25-27 AMP	Philippians 4:8 TLB
Hebrews 9:14 NIV	Proverbs 4:23 AMP

1 Thessalonians 4:8 AMP   1 John 3:1-3 AMP
James 3:17 NIV   Revelation 12:11

I.

A Man of Purity

Father, I attend to Your Word. I hide it in my heart that I might not sin against You. It is not wrong to have sexual desires — You made me, You know me, and You bought me — I belong to You. I commit myself and all my natural affections to You, Father, and acknowledge the power of the Holy Spirit in my life. I give Him control, and submit to Your will.

Forgive me for sinning against You, against myself, and against others. Thank You for Your grace that enables me to leave my gift at the altar when I remember that someone has a grievance against me. I will go and make peace with that person whenever possible, and then come back and present my gift to You.

In the name of Jesus, I thank You for the power to shun immorality and all sexual looseness. I [flee from impurity in thought, word, or deed]. My body is the temple (the very sanctuary) of the Holy Spirit Who lives within me, Whom I have received [as a Gift] from You. I am not my own. I was bought with a price [purchased with a preciousness and paid for, made Your own]. So then, I will honor You, Father, and bring glory to You in my body.

When I read Your Word, I receive the truth that makes me free. I have won my battle with Satan. I have learned to know You as my Father. I am strong with Your Word in my heart. I no longer love this evil world and all that it offers me, for when I love these things I show that I do not really love You, Lord; for all these worldly things, these evil desires — the craze for sex, the ambition to buy everything that appeals to me, and the pride that comes from wealth and importance — these are not from You, Father. They are from this evil world itself. This world is fading away, and these evil, forbidden things will go with it, but whoever keeps doing Your will, Lord, will live forever.

Thank You, Father, that I have been anointed by [I hold a sacred appointment from, and I have been given an unction from] the Holy One, and I know [the truth]. I have received the Holy Spirit, and He lives within me, in my heart, so that I don't need anyone to teach me what is right. For He teaches me all things, and He is the Truth, and no liar; and so, just as He has said, I must live in Christ, never to depart from Him.

O Father, I stay in happy fellowship with You so that when Your Son Jesus comes I will be sure that all is well and will not have to be ashamed and shrink back from meeting Him. I know that You are always good and do only right, and I seek to be an imitator of You, and do what is good and right.

In Jesus' name, amen.

Scripture References

Proverbs 4:20	1 John 2:12-17 TLB
Psalm 119:11	1 John 2:20,27-29 TLB
Matthew 5:23,24 AMP	Matthew 6:33 AMP
1 Corinthians 6:18-20 AMP	Ephesians 5:1 AMP
John 8:32 AMP	

II.

A Woman of Purity

Father, on the authority of Your Word I declare and decree that I am a new creation in Christ. I repent of my former sins, receive Your forgiveness, and renew my mind — replacing old thought patterns and habits with Your thoughts and plans for me.

I was a sinner, separated, (living apart) from Christ. But now in Christ Jesus, my Lord, I have been brought near through the blood of Christ. I confess that Jesus is my Lord and believe in my heart that You raised Him from the dead. Therefore, I am ingrafted in Christ (the Messiah). Now, today, I am a new creation (a new creature altogether); the old [previous moral and spiritual condition] has passed away. Behold, the fresh and new has come!

Since I have confidence to enter the Most Holy Place by the blood of Jesus, by a new and living way opened for me through the curtain, that is, His body, and since I have a great priest over the house of God, I draw near to You, Lord, with a sincere heart in full assurance of faith, having my heart sprinkled to cleanse me from a guilty conscience and having my body washed with pure water. I hold unswervingly to the hope I profess, for He Who promised is faithful. And I consider how I may spur others on toward love and good deeds. I will not give up meeting together, as some are in the habit of doing, but I will encourage others, and all the more as I see the Day approaching.

Father, I am Your daughter (Your handmaiden), and You have poured out Your Spirit upon me, and I shall prophesy [telling forth the divine counsels and predicting future events pertaining especially to Your Kingdom]. I seek (aim at and strive after) first of all Your Kingdom and Your righteousness (Your way of doing and being right), and then all these things taken together will be given me besides. I will not worry or be anxious about tomorrow, for tomorrow will have worries and anxieties of its own. Sufficient for each day is its own trouble.

As Your daughter, I thank You for enduing me with Your grace (free, spontaneous, absolute favor and loving-kindness). With You, Father, nothing is ever impossible, and no word from You shall be without power or impossible of fulfillment.

Father, I submit to Your will for my life. Your ways are higher than my ways, Your thoughts higher than my thoughts. I commit my way to You and You will cause my thoughts to become agreeable to Your will and so shall my plans be established and succeed. I am Your handmaid; let it be done to me according to Your Word.

Since I have such a huge crowd of men and women of faith watching me from the grandstands, I strip off anything that slows me down or holds me back, and especially those sins that wrap themselves so tightly around my feet and trip me up; and I run with patience the particular race that You have set before me. I keep my eyes on Jesus, my Leader and Instructor.

Father, to the pure You show Yourself pure, and to the willful You show Yourself willful. The afflicted people You will deliver, but Your eyes are upon the haughty, whom You will bring down. For You, O Lord, are my Lamp; You, Lord lighten my darkness. For by

You I run through a troop; by You I leap over a wall. As for You, Lord, Your way is perfect; Your Word is tried. You are my Shield for I trust and take refuge in You.

O Father, that I might ascend the hill of the Lord, and stand in Your holy place. I come with clean hands and a pure heart, refusing to lift up my soul to an idol or swear by what is false that I may receive blessing and vindication from You, my God and my Savior. Surely, Lord God, You are good to those who are pure in heart.

In Jesus' name I pray, amen.

Scripture References

2 Corinthians 5:17	Luke 1:28,30,37 AMP
Romans 12:1,2 AMP	Isaiah 55:9 AMP
Jeremiah 29:11 AMP	Proverbs 16:3 AMP
Ephesians 2:12,13 AMP	Luke 1:38 AMP
Romans 10:9	Hebrews 12:1,2 TLB
2 Corinthians 5:17 AMP	2 Samuel 22:27-31 AMP
Hebrews 10:19-25 NIV	Psalm 24:3-5 NIV
Acts 2:17 AMP	Psalm 73:1 NIV
Matthew 6:33,34 AMP	

Letting Go of Bitterness

Introduction

In interviews with divorced men and women, I have been encouraged to write a prayer on overcoming bitterness.

Often, the injustice of the situation in which these people find themselves creates deep hurts, wounds in the spirit, and anger that is so near the surface the individuals involved risk sinking into the trap of bitterness and revenge. Their thoughts may turn inward as they consider the unfairness of the situation and dwell on how badly they have been treated.

In a family divorce situation, bitterness sometimes distorts ideas of what is best for the child/children involved. One parent (and sometimes both parents) will use the child/children against the other.

Unresolved anger often moves one marriage partner to hurt the one he or she holds responsible for the hurt and sense of betrayal which they feel.

There is healing available. There is a way of escape for all who will turn to the Healer, obeying Him and trusting Him.

Prayer

Father, life seems so unjust, so unfair. The pain of rejection is almost more than I can bear. My past relationships have ended in strife, anger, rejection, and separation.

Lord, help me to let go of all bitterness and indignation and wrath (passion, rage, bad temper) and resentment (anger, animosity).

You are the One Who binds up and heals the brokenhearted. I receive Your anointing that destroys every yoke of bondage. I receive emotional healing by faith, and I thank You for giving me the grace to stand firm until the process is complete.

Thank You for wise counselors. I acknowledge the Holy Spirit as my wonderful Counselor. Thank You for helping me work out my salvation with fear and trembling, for it is You, Father, Who work in me to will and to act according to Your good purpose.

In the name of Jesus, I choose to forgive those who have wronged me. I purpose to live a life of forgiveness because You have forgiven me. With the help of the Holy Spirit, I get rid of all bitterness, rage, and anger, brawling and slander, along with every form of malice. I desire to be kind and compassionate to others, forgiving them, just as in Christ You forgave me.

With the help of the Holy Spirit, I make every effort to live in peace with all men and to be holy, for I know that without holiness no one will see You, Lord. I purpose to see to it that I do not miss Your grace and that no bitter root grows up within me to cause trouble and defile me.

I will watch and pray that I enter not into temptation or cause others to stumble.

Thank You, Father, that You watch over Your Word to perform it and that whom the Son has set free is free indeed. I declare that I have overcome resentment and bitterness by the blood of the Lamb, and by the word of my testimony.

In Jesus' name, amen.

Scripture References

Ephesians 4:31 AMP   Ephesians 4:31,32 NIV

Luke 4:18   Hebrews 12:14,15 NIV

Isaiah 10:27   Matthew 26:41

Proverbs 11:14   Romans 14:21

John 15:26 AMP   Jeremiah 1:12 AMP

Philippians 2:12,13 NIV   John 8:36

Matthew 5:44   Revelation 12:11

Husbands

Father, in the name of Jesus, I take Your Word and confess this day that I hearken to Your wisdom. My wife and I dwell securely in confident trust, and we are without fear or dread of evil. I make my ears attentive to skillful and godly wisdom, inclining and directing my heart and mind to understanding. I apply all of my power to the quest of wisdom and understanding.

I let not mercy, kindness, and truth forsake me. I bind them about my neck and write them on the tablet of my heart. I prize the wisdom of God highly and exalt her. She will exalt and promote me, bringing me honor because I embrace her. For You, Lord, are my confidence, firm and strong, and You keep my foot from being caught in a trap or hidden danger.

Where I go, the Word of God shall lead me. When I sleep, it shall keep me. When I awaken, it shall talk to me. Therefore, I will speak excellent and princely things, and the opening of my lips shall be for right things. All the words of my mouth are righteous — upright and in right standing with God — and there is nothing contrary to truth or crooked in them.

I live considerately with my wife, with an intelligent recognition of our marriage relationship. I honor my wife as physically the weaker. However, I realize that we are joint-heirs to the throne with Jesus spiritually. I do this in order that our prayers will not be hindered or cut off.

I confess that my wife and I are of one and the same mind, united in spirit, compassionate and courteous, tenderhearted and humble-minded. I believe for our welfare, happiness, and protection, because we love and respect each other.

Father, thank You that we are a couple of good report, that we are successful in everything we set our hands to. We are uncompromisingly righteous. We capture human lives for You as fishers of men. As we do this, we are confident that You are the Lord God Who teaches us to profit and leads us in the way we should go. We are abundantly supplied, with every need met, in the name of Jesus. We have obtained the favor of the Lord, and the will of God is done in our lives and in our children's lives. Amen.

Scripture References

Proverbs 1:33	Proverbs 2:2
Proverbs 3:3	Proverbs 4:8
Proverbs 3:26	Proverbs 6:22
Proverbs 8:6,8	1 Peter 3:7-9
Proverbs 11:30	Isaiah 48:17

Wives

Father, in the name of Jesus, I take Your Word and speak it out of my mouth and say that I have faith that I am a capable, intelligent, patient, and virtuous woman. I am far more precious than jewels. My value to my husband and family is far above rubies and pearls.

The heart of my husband trusts in me confidently and relies on and believes in me completely, so that he has no lack of honest gain or need of dishonest spoil.

Father, I will comfort, encourage, and do him only good as long as there is life within me. I gird myself with strength and spiritual, mental, and physical fitness for my God-given task. I taste and see that my gain from work with and for God is good. My lamp goes not out; it burns on continually through the night of any trouble, privation, or sorrow, and it warns away fear, doubt, and distrust.

I open my hand to the poor. I reach out my filled hands to the needy — whether in spirit, soul, or body.

PRAYERS THAT AVAIL MUCH COMMEMORATIVE GIFT EDITION

My husband is known as a success in everything he puts his hand to. Strength and dignity are my clothing, and my position in my household is strong. I am secure and at peace in knowing that my family is in readiness for the future.

I open my mouth with skillful and Godly wisdom, and in my tongue is the law of kindness and love. I look well to how things go in my household. The bread of idleness, gossip, discontent, and self-pity I will not eat.

My children rise up and call me blessed and happy. My husband boasts of and praises me, saying that I excel in all that I set my hand to. I am a woman who reverently and worshipfully loves You, Lord, and You shall give me the fruits of my hands. My works will praise me wherever I go, for Father, I confess that I am a submitted wife — simply because I want to be and I recognize Your authority. I thank You for my husband who is head over me, but who has given me (through the chain of command) the necessary power to do what Your Word says for me to do from Proverbs 31:10-31. I

am as this woman is — a loving, successful, submitted
wife — in the name of Jesus. Amen.

Scripture References (AMP)

Proverbs 31:10-31

Compatibility in Marriage

Father, in the name of Jesus, I pray and confess that my spouse and I endure long and are patient and kind; that we are never envious and never boil over with jealousy. We are not boastful or vainglorious, and we do not display ourselves haughtily. We are not conceited or arrogant and inflated with pride. We are not rude and unmannerly, and we do not act unbecomingly. We do not insist on our own rights or our own way, for we are not self-seeking or touchy or fretful or resentful. We take no account of the evil done to us and pay no attention to a suffered wrong. We do not rejoice at injustice and unrighteousness, but we rejoice when right and truth prevail.

We bear up under anything and everything that comes. We are ever ready to believe the best of each other. Our hopes are fadeless under all circumstances. We endure everything without weakening. *Our love never fails* — it never fades out or becomes obsolete or comes to an end.

When Desiring To Have a Baby

Our Father, my spouse and I bow our knees unto You. Father of our Lord Jesus Christ of Whom the whole family in heaven and on earth is named, we pray that You would grant to us according to the riches of Your glory, to be strengthened with might by Your Spirit in the inner man. Christ dwells in our hearts by faith, that we — being rooted and grounded in love — may be able to comprehend with all the saints what is the breadth, and length, and depth, and height of the love of Christ, which passes knowledge, that we might be filled with all the fullness of God.

Hallelujah, we praise You, O Lord, for You give children to the childless wife, so that she becomes a happy mother. And we thank You that You are the One Who is building our family. As Your children and inheritors through Jesus Christ, we receive Your gift — the fruit of the womb, Your child as our reward.

We praise You, our Father, in Jesus' name, for we know that whatsoever we ask, we receive of You, because we keep Your commandments, and do those things which are pleasing in Your sight.

Thank You, Father, that we are a fruitful vine within our house; our children will be like olive shoots around our table. Thus shall we be blessed because we fear the Lord.

In Jesus' name we pray, amen.

Scripture References

Ephesians 3:14-19   1 John 3:22,23 AMP

Psalm 113:9 AMP   Psalm 128:3,4 AMP

Psalm 127:3

The Unborn Child

Father, in Jesus' name, I thank You for my unborn child. I treasure this child as a gift from You. My child was created in Your image, perfectly healthy and complete. You have known my child since conception and know the path he/she will take with his/her life. I ask Your blessing upon him/her and stand and believe in his/her salvation through Jesus Christ.

When You created man and woman, You called them blessed and crowned them with glory and honor. It is in You, Father, that my child will live and move, and have his/her being. He/she is Your offspring and will come to worship and praise You.

Heavenly Father, I thank and praise You for the great things You have done and are continuing to do. I am in awe at the miracle of life You have placed inside of me. Thank You! Amen.

Scripture References

Psalm 127:3   Matthew 18:18

Genesis 1:26

Jeremiah 1:5

2 Peter 3:9

Psalm 8:5

Acts 17:28,29

John 14:13

Galatians 3:13

1 John 3:8

Psalm 91:1

Godly Order in Pregnancy and Childbirth

Father, in Jesus' name, I confess Your Word this day over my pregnancy and the birth of my child. I ask that You will quickly perform Your Word trusting that it will not go out from You and return to You void, but rather that it will accomplish that which pleases You. Your Word is quick and powerful, and discerns my heart intentions and the thoughts of my mind.

Right now I put on the whole armor of God so that I may be able to stand against the tricks and traps of the devil. I recognize that my fight is not with flesh and blood, but against principalities, powers and the rulers of darkness and spiritual wickedness in high places. God, I stand above all, taking the shield of faith and being able to quench the attacks of the devil with Your mighty power. I stand in faith during this pregnancy and birth, not giving any room to fear, but possessing power, love and a sound mind as Your Word promises in 2 Timothy 1:7.

Heavenly Father, I confess that You are my refuge; I trust You during this pregnancy and childbirth. I am thankful that You have put angels at watch over me and my unborn child. I cast all the care and burden of this pregnancy over on You, Lord. Your grace is sufficient for me through this pregnancy; You strengthen my weaknesses.

Father, Your Word declares that my unborn child was created in Your image, fearfully and wonderfully made to praise You. You have made me a joyful mother, and I am blessed with a heritage from You as my reward. I commit this child to You, Father, and pray that he will grow and call me blessed.

I am not afraid of pregnancy or childbirth because I am fixed and trusting upon You, Father. I believe that my pregnancy and childbirth will be void of all problems. Thank You, Father, that all decisions regarding my pregnancy and delivery will be godly, that the Holy Spirit will intervene. Lord, You are my dwelling place and I rest in the knowledge that evil will not come near me and no sickness or infirmity will strike me or my unborn child. I know that Jesus died on the cross to take

away my sickness and pain. Having accepted Your Son
Jesus as my Savior, I confess that my child will be born
healthy and completely whole. Thank You, Father, for
the law of the Spirit of life in Christ Jesus that has made
me and my child free from the law of sin and death!

Father, thank You for protecting me and my baby
and for our good health. Thank You for hearing and
answering my prayers. Amen.

Scripture References

Jeremiah 1:12	Proberbs 31:28
Isaiah 55:11	Psalm 112:7
Hebrews 4:12	Psalm 91:1,10
Ephesians 6:11,12,16	Matthew 8:17
Psalm 91:2,11	Romans 8:2
1 Peter 5:7	James 4:7
2 Corinthians 12:9	Ephesians 6:12
Genesis 1:26	John 4:13
Psalm 139:14	Matthew 18:18
Psalm 113:9	Jeremiah 33:3
Psalm 127:3	

Adopting a Child

Father, in Jesus' name, we come boldly before Your throne of grace that we may receive mercy and find grace to help in our time of need. We are trusting in You, and seek to do good; so that we may dwell in the land, and feed surely on Your faithfulness.

We delight ourselves also in You, and You give us the desires and secret petitions of our heart. We believe our desire to adopt a child is from You, and we are willing to assume the responsibility of rearing this child in the ways of the Master.

Father, we commit our way to You [roll and repose each care of our load on You]. Our confidence is in You, and You will bring this adoption to pass according to Your purpose and plan.

Lord, Your Son Jesus demonstrated Your love for children when He said, ..."**Let the children alone, don't prevent them from coming to me. God's kingdom is**

made up of people like these" (Matt. 19:14 MESSAGE).
Then, He laid hands on them and blessed them.

Use us as Your instruments of peace and righteousness to bless this child. We purpose in our hearts to train this child up in the way that he/she should go.

Lord, we are embracing this child (Your best gift) as our very own with Your love, as Jesus said, **"Whoever embraces one of these children as I do embraces me, and far more than me — God who sent me"** (Mark 9:37 MESSAGE).

Father, take this child up and be a Father and Mother to him/her as we extend our hands and our hearts to embrace him/her. Thank You for the blood of Jesus that gives protection to this one whom we love.

We thank You for the man and woman who conceived this child, and pray that You will bless them, cause Your face to shine upon them, and be merciful to them. If they do not know Jesus, we ask You, the Lord of the harvest, to send forth laborers to share truth with them that they may come out of the snare of the devil.

Mercy and truth are written upon the tablets of our hearts, and You cause us to find favor and good understanding with You and with man — the adoption agency staff, the judges, and all those who are involved in this decision-making process. May everyone be careful that they do not despise one of these little ones over whom they have jurisdiction — for they have angels who see Your face continually in heaven.

We believe that all our words are righteous (upright and in right standing with You, Father). By our long forbearing and calmness of spirit those in authority are persuaded, and our soft speech breaks down the most bonelike resistance.

Lord, we are looking to You as our Great Counselor and Mighty Advocate. We ask for Your wisdom for us and our attorneys.

Father, contend with those who contend with us, and give safety to our child and ease him/her day by day. We are calling on You, in the name of Jesus, and You will answer us and show us great and mighty things. No weapon formed against us and this adoption shall prosper, and any tongue that rises against us in judgment we shall show to be in the wrong. This [peace, righteousness, security, and triumph over opposition] is our inheritance as Your children.

Father, we believe, therefore we have spoken. May it be done unto us according to Your Word.

In Jesus' name, amen.

Scripture References

Hebrews 4:16   Matthew 18:10 PHILLIPS

Psalm 37:3   Proverbs 8:8 AMP

Psalm 37:4 AMP   Proverbs 25:15 AMP

Ephesians 6:4 MESSAGE   James 1:5

Psalm 37:5 AMP   Isaiah 49:25

Proverbs 22:6   Jeremiah 33:3

Psalm 67:1   Isaiah 54:17 AMP

Matthew 9:38   Psalm 116:10

2 Timothy 2:26   Luke 1:38

Proverbs 3:3,4

The Children

Father, in the name of Jesus, I pray and confess Your Word over my children and surround them with my faith — faith in Your Word that You watch over it to perform it! I confess and believe that my children are disciples of Christ taught of the Lord and obedient to Your will. Great is the peace and undisturbed composure of my children, because You, God, contend with that which contends with my children, and You give them safety and ease them.

Father, You will perfect that which concerns me. *I commit and cast the care of my children once and for all over on You, Father.* They are in Your hands, and I am positively persuaded that You are able to guard and keep that which I have committed to You. You are more than enough!

I confess that my children obey their parents in the Lord as His representatives, because this is just and right. My children _____ honor, esteem, and value as precious their parents; for this is the first

Blessing the Household

Introduction

As the head of the family, it is your privilege and duty to pray for the household in your charge and those under your care and authority.

The following prayer was written to be prayed by a man or a woman. So often, in today's society, the woman finds herself having to assume the responsibility and position of the head of the household.

I.

Prayer of Blessing for the Household

Father, as the priest and head of this household, I declare and decree, "As for me and my house, we shall serve the Lord."

Praise be to You, the God and Father of our Lord Jesus Christ, for You have blessed us in the heavenly realms with every spiritual blessing in Christ. We reverence You and worship You in spirit and in truth.

Lord, we acknowledge and welcome the presence of Your Holy Spirit here in our home. We thank You, Father, that Your Son Jesus is here with us because we are gathered together in His name.

Lord God, Your divine power has given us everything we need for life and godliness through our knowledge of You Who called us by Your own glory and goodness.

As spiritual leader of this home, I declare on the authority of Your Word that my family will be mighty in the land; this generation of the upright will be blessed.

Father, You delight in the prosperity of Your people; and we thank You that wealth and riches are in our house, and our righteousness endures forever.

In the name of Jesus, amen.

Scripture References

Revelation 1:6	2 Peter 1:3 NIV
Joshua 24:15	Psalm 112:2 NIV
Ephesians 1:3 NIV	Psalm 25:37

John 4:23   Psalm 112:3

Matthew 18:20

II.

Prayer of Blessing at the Table

Introduction

This prayer was written for the head of the house-hold to pray not only to thank and praise God for His blessings, but also to cleanse and consecrate the food received and to sanctify the family members who partake of it.

Prayer

Father, thank You for giving to us our daily bread. We receive this food with thanksgiving and praise. You bless our bread and our water and take sickness out of the midst of us.

In the name of Jesus, we call this food clean, whole-some, and pure, nourishment to our bodies. Should there be any deadly thing herein, it shall not harm us for the Spirit of life in Christ Jesus makes us free from the law of sin and death.

In the name of Jesus, amen.

Scripture References

Matthew 6:11	Mark 16:18
1 Timothy 4:4 NIV	Romans 8:2
Exodus 23:25	

III.

Husband's Prayer of Blessing for His Wife
Introduction

It is positive reinforcement, validation, and affirmation for children to hear their father pray, blessing his wife and their mother. This is a method of honoring her and reaffirming her position in the home. Words are powerful, and the blessings for the wife in front of the children will promote appropriate self-esteem necessary for success in life.

Sometimes, a wife will feel that she has failed because she is not fulfilling all the roles expressed in Proverbs 31. I believe that God had this passage written to encourage a woman to be all that He created her to be. Out of her "being" — knowing herself, both her strengths and her weaknesses, developing her talents, seeing herself as God sees her, and looking to Christ for her completeness (wholeness) — comes the "doing."

"The woman described in this chapter has outstanding abilities. Her family's social position is high. In fact, she may not be one woman at all — she may be a composite portrait of ideal womanhood. Do not see her as a model to imitate in every detail; your days are not long enough to do everything she does! See her instead as an inspiration to be all you can be. We can't be just like her, but we can learn from her industry, integrity, and resourcefulness."[1]

---

[1] *Life Application Bible*, New International Version edition (Wheaton, IL: Tyndale House Publishers, 1988, 1989, 1990, 1991), commentary at bottom of p. 1131.

Prayer

Father, I thank You for my wife who is a capable, intelligent, and virtuous woman. Her worth is far more precious than jewels, and her value is far above rubies or pearls.

I thank You that she is a woman of strong character, great wisdom, many skills, and great compassion. Strength and dignity are her clothing, and her position is strong and secure. She opens her mouth with skillful and godly wisdom, and on her tongue is the law of kindness [giving counsel and instruction].

Our children rise up and call her blessed (happy, fortunate, and to be envied); and I boast of and praise her, [saying], "Many daughters have done virtuously, nobly, and well [with the strength of character that is steadfast in goodness], but you excel them all."

Father, my wife reverently and worshipfully fears You, she shall be praised! Give her of the fruit of her hands, and let her own works praise her in the gates [of the city].

I respect, value, and honor my wife before our children.

In the name of Jesus, amen.

Scripture References (AMP)

Proverbs 31:10	Proverbs 31:28,29
Proverbs 31:25,26	Proverbs 31:30,31

IV.

Parent's Prayer of Blessing for Children

Introduction

"The [Hebrew] father's place in the [traditional Jewish] home is fittingly shown by the beautiful custom of blessing the children, a custom which dates back to Isaac and Jacob. To this day, in many homes, the father blesses his children on Friday nights, on Rosh Hashanah eve and on Yom Kippur before leaving for the synagogue....

"In very ancient times, the father or patriarch was the ruler of home and family. He made laws and enforced them. Later, however, laws were instituted by teachers, parents, judges and kings. The father, as the master of the house, was looked up to for support and depended on for guidance."[2]

The following prayer, based on a translation of the traditional Hebrew father's blessing upon his children, may be used by the head of the household, whether male or female.

Prayer

Father, I receive, welcome, and acknowledge each of my children as a delightful blessing from You. I speak Your blessings upon them and over them.

Children, I bless you in the name of Jesus, proclaiming the blessings of God, my Redeemer, upon you. May He give you wisdom, a reverential fear of God, and a heart of love.

May He create in you the desire to attend to His words; a willing and obedient heart that you may

---

[2] Ben M. Edidin, *Jewish Customs and Ceremonies* (New York: Hebrew Publishing Company, 1941), p. 23.

consent and submit to His sayings and walk in His ways. May your eyes look straight ahead with purpose for the future. May your tongue be as the pen of a ready writer, writing mercy and kindness upon the tablets of your heart. May you speak the truth in love. May your hands do the works of the Father; may your feet walk the paths which He has foreordained for you.

I have no greater joy than this, to hear that my children are living their lives in the truth.

May the Lord prepare you and your future mate to love and honor one another, and may He grant to your union upright sons and daughters who will live in accordance with His Word. May your source of livelihood be honorable and secure, so that you will earn a living with your own hands. May you always worship God in spirit and in truth.

I pray above all things that you may always prosper and be in health even as your soul prospers. ...**I know the thoughts and plans that I have for you, says the Lord, thoughts and plans for welfare and peace and not** for evil, to give you hope in your final outcome (Jer. 29:11 AMP).

In the name of Jesus, amen.

Scripture References

Psalm 127:3 AMP	Ephesians 2:10 AMP
Philippians 2:13 AMP	3 John 4 AMP
Proverbs 4:20	1 Thessalonians 4:11,12 NIV
Psalm 45:1	John 4:23
Proverbs 3:3 AMP	3 John 2
Ephesians 4:15	

Peace in the Family

Father, in the name of Jesus, I thank You that You have poured Your Spirit upon our family from on high. Our wilderness has become a fruitful field, and we value our fruitful field as a forest. Justice dwells in our wilderness, and righteousness [religious and moral rectitude in every area and relation] abides in our fruitful field. The effect of righteousness is peace [internal and external], and the result of righteousness, quietness and confident trust forever.

Our family dwells in a peaceable habitation, in safe dwellings and in quiet resting places. And there is stability in our times, abundance of salvation, wisdom and knowledge. There, reverent fear and worship of the Lord is our treasure and Yours.

O Lord, be gracious to us; we have waited [expectantly] for You. Be the arm of Your servants — our strength and defense — every morning, our salvation in the time of trouble.

Father, we thank You for our peace, our safety and our welfare this day. Hallelujah! Amen.

Scripture References (AMP)

Isaiah 32:15-18   Isaiah 33:2,6

Handling Household Finances

Introduction

The following prayers may be prayed individually or as a couple. In preparation for marriage it is great wisdom for the couple to discuss finances. Each party comes with an individual view of how to handle money — spending and/or saving. It is wise to set up a budget that is agreeable to both.

There is a danger in the tendency to assume that the other party has the same opinions and ideas about money or, in case of disagreement, that one's own way is right and the other person's is wrong. Financial differences is one of Satan's greatest weapons for introducing strife and bringing pressure to bear on a marriage. Spending money can quickly evolve into an emotional experience, causing many other problems.

God is *El Shaddai*, God Almighty (Ex. 6:3 AMP) — the God Who is more than enough — and His intention is that His children enjoy good health and that all may go well with them, even as their soul is getting along well. (3 John 2 NIV.) Two people coming into agreement with God's financial plan will offset the enemy's schemes to divide and conquer.

If you and your beloved are planning to marry, or to establish a financial plan in your existing marriage, listen to one another. Understand what each other is saying. Realize that there are differences in viewpoints about money and allow for those differences. Determine who is more astute in financial matters: balancing the checkbook, paying the bills on time, and making wise investments. Set aside time in your schedule to keep each other informed, review goals, and make plans. Wisdom from above is willing to yield to reason; cooperate one with the other. (James 3:17 AMP.)

Prayer

Father, we come before You in the name of Jesus. Thank You for the Holy Spirit Who is present with us as we discuss our financial future together. We thank You for bringing us to this place in our lives. You have started a good work in us and will perform it until the day of Christ. We welcome You as we prepare to set up a budget that is pleasing to You and to each of us.

Jesus is our Lord and our High Priest, and we purpose to bring Him the firstfruits of our income and worship You, the Lord our God, with them.

Father, You are Lord over our marriage — over this union that we believe has been ordained by You. We confess Your Word over our life together and our finances. As we do so, we say that Your Word will not return to You void, but will accomplish what it says it will do.

Therefore, we believe in the name of Jesus that all our needs are met, according to Your riches in glory. We acknowledge You as Lord over our finances by giving tithes and offerings to further Your cause.

Father, on the authority of Your Word we declare that gifts will be given to us; good measure, pressed down, and shaken together, and running over shall they be poured into our bosom. For with the same measure we deal out, it shall be measured back to us.

We remember that it is written in Your Word that he who sows sparingly and grudgingly will also reap sparingly and grudgingly, and he who sows generously [that blessings may come to someone] will also reap generously and with blessings.

Lord, remind us always, and we purpose to remember, that it is You Who give us power to become rich, and You do it to fulfill Your promise to our ancestors. We will never feel that it was our own power and might that made us wealthy.

Father, not only do we give tithes and offerings to You, but we also give to those around us who are in need. Your Word also says that he who gives to the poor lends to You and You pay wonderful interest on the loan! We acknowledge You as we give for the benefit of the poor.

Thank You, Father, that as You bless us and we bless others, they will praise You and give You thanks and bless others and the circle of Your love and blessing will go on and on into eternity.

In the name of Jesus we pray, amen.

Scripture References

John 14:17

Philippians 1:6

Hebrews 3:1

Deuteronomy 26:10,11

Isaiah 55:11

Philippians 4:19

Luke 6:38

2 Corinthians 9:6 AMP

Deuteronomy 8:17,18 TLB

Proverbs 19:17 TLB

2 Corinthians 9:12-15 AMP,

NIV, PHILLIPS

I.

Setting Aside the Tithe

Father, Your Word states, **Be sure to set aside a tenth of all that your fields produce each year....so that you may learn to revere the Lord Your God always** (Deut. 14:22,23 NIV). We purpose to set aside the tithe because it belongs to You, O God our Father.

It is our delight to bring all the tithes (the whole tenth of our income) into the storehouse, that there may be food in Your house. Lord of hosts, in accordance with Your Word, we prove You now by paying You the tithe. You are opening the windows of heaven for us and pouring us out a blessing, that there shall not be room enough to receive it.

Thank You, Father, for rebuking the devourer for our sakes; he shall not destroy the fruits of our ground, neither shall our vine drop its fruit before the time in the field.

We praise You, Lord, for recording our names in Your book of remembrance of those who reverence and worshipfully fear You and who think on Your name so that we may be Yours in the day when You publicly recognize and openly declare us to be Your jewels (Your special possession, Your peculiar treasure).

Thank You for bringing us out of the authority of darkness and translating us into the Kingdom of Your dear Son, Jesus Christ, our Lord.

In His name we pray, amen.

Scripture References

Malachi 3:10,11 AMP   Colossians 1:13
Malachi 3:16,17 AMP

II.

Giving the Offering

Father, we give offerings at the direction of the Holy Spirit. We are ever ready with a generous and willing gift. At Your instructions we remember this: he who sows sparingly and grudgingly will also reap sparingly and grudgingly, and he who sows generously [that blessings may come to someone] will also reap generously and with blessings.

We [give] as we make up our own mind and purpose in our hearts, not reluctantly or sorrowfully or under compulsion, for You, Lord, love (take pleasure in, prize above other things, and are unwilling to abandon or to do without) a cheerful (joyous "prompt to do it") giver [whose heart is in his giving].

Father, we thank You that You are able to make all grace (every favor and earthly blessing) come to us in abundance, so that we may always and under all circumstances and whatever the need be self-sufficient [possessing enough to require no aid or support and furnished in abundance for every good work and charitable donation].

Father, [You] provide seed for our sowing and bread for our eating. Thank You for providing and multiplying [our resources], for sowing and increasing the fruits of our righteousness. Thus we will be enriched in all things and in every way, so that we can be generous, and [our generosity as it is] administered by us will bring forth thanksgiving to You.

We confess with the psalmist David, we have not seen the righteous forsaken, nor his seed begging bread.

We thank You for food, clothing, and shelter. In the name of Jesus, we determine to stop being perpetually uneasy (anxious and worried) about our life together, what we shall eat and what we shall drink, or about our bodies, what we shall put on. Our life — individually and together — is greater [in quality] than food, and our bodies [far above and more excellent] than clothing.

The bread of idleness [gossip, discontent, and self-pity] we will not eat. We declare on the authority of

Your Word that our family will be mighty in the land: this generation of the upright will be blessed.

Father, You delight in the prosperity of Your people; and we thank You that wealth and riches are in our house, and our righteousness endures forever.

Good comes to us for we are generous and lend freely, and conduct our affairs with justice. When we lack wisdom, we will ask of You, and You will give generously without finding fault with us.

In the name of Jesus, amen.

Scripture References

2 Corinthians 9:5-11 AMP   Psalm 112:2,3

Psalm 37:25   Psalm 37:26 NIV

Matthew 6:25 AMP   2 Corinthians 9:9 AMP

Proverbs 31:27 AMP   James 1:5 NIV

Psalm 35:27

Moving to a New Location

Father, Your Word says that You will perfect that which concerns us. Your mercy and loving-kindness, O Lord, endure forever — forsake not the works of Your own hands. We bring to You our apprehensions concerning our relocation. We ask You to go before us to make the crooked places straight in finding a new home.

Give us wisdom to make wise decisions in choosing the movers and packers best suited to handle our possessions. We have favor, good understanding, and high esteem in the sight of You and man — with the utility companies, with the school systems, and with the banks — with everyone involved in this move.

Father, we thank You for supplying and preparing the new friends that You would want us to have. We are trusting You to direct us to a church where we can fellowship with like believers, in one accord, where we are free to worship and praise You and sing to You a new song.

Father, in the name of Jesus, we commit this move to You, knowing that You provide for Your children. We not unto our own understanding, but in all our ways we acknowledge You, and You shall direct our paths.

Thank You, Father, for Your blessing on this move.

In the name of Jesus, amen.

Scripture References

Psalm 138:8	Psalm 40:3
Isaiah 45:2	Psalm 96:1
James 1:5	Psalm 98:1
Proverbs 3:4	Psalm 149:1
Hebrews 10:25	Psalm 37:4,5
Acts 2:1,46	Philippians 4:6,7
Acts 4:34	Isaiah 26:3
Philippians 2:2	Proverbs 3:5,6
Isaiah 42:10	

trust You and delight ourselves in You, and You will give us the desires of our hearts.

We make all these requests known unto You with thanksgiving, and the peace that passes all understanding shall guard our hearts and minds. You will keep us in perfect peace because our minds are stayed on You. We trust in You, Father, with all our hearts. We lean

and

mischief a

fraud and guile do not dep

marketplaces. I am calling upon You, Lord, and You will save me and my household as well.

Father, in the name of Jesus, You and You alone are our safety and our protection. My household and I are looking to You, for our strength comes from You — the God Who made heaven and earth. You will not let us stumble. You are our Guardian God Who will not fall asleep. You are right at our side to protect us. You guard us from every evil, You guard our very lives. You guard us when we leave and when we return. You guard us now; You guard us always.

My household was chosen and foreknown by You, Father, and consecrated (sanctified, made holy) by the Spirit to be obedient to Jesus Christ (the Messiah) and to be sprinkled with [His] blood. We receive grace (spiritual blessing) and peace in ever increasing abundance [that spiritual peace to be realized in and through Christ, freedom from fears, agitating passions, and moral conflicts].

Lord, Your Son Jesus became our Passover by shedding His own precious blood. He is the Mediator (the Go-between, Agent) of a new covenant, and His sprinkled blood speaks of mercy. On the authority of Your Word, I proclaim that the blood of Jesus is our protection, as it is written, ...**when I see the blood, I will pass over you...** (Ex. 12:13). I declare and decree that I am drawing a blood-line around my children, and the evil one cannot cross it.

I know that none of the God-begotten make a practice of sin — fatal sin. The God-begotten are also the God-protected. The evil one can't lay a hand on my household. I know that we are held firm by You, Lord.

Father, thank You for Your divine protection. In the name of Jesus I pray, amen.[1]

Scripture References

1 John 3:1   Psalm 121:1-8 MESSAGE

1 Peter 1:18,19   1 Peter 1:2 AMP

1 John 2:12   Hebrews 12:24 AMP

Psalm 123:4 AMP   1 John 5:18,19 MESSAGE

Psalm 55:9-11,16 AMP

---

[1] In addition to praying this prayer, read Psalm 91 aloud over your family each day.

Dealing With an Abusive Family Situation

Introduction

In our ministry, we receive letters from women who are living in abusive situations. Since many of them do not feel or believe that they can leave, they request that we write prayers to cover this area of need. They are fearful of practicing tough love. A need for security plays a big role in their decision to remain where they are. Or, in certain cases they fear increased or even more severe abuse should they try to leave. Others have asked the abuser to leave or have moved out themselves. Yet, their request is for prayer for deliverance for the abuser and other family members.

When I am traveling, I often meet women who feel that it is safe to talk with me. At the close of a meeting, a few years ago, I was approached by an attractive woman whom I recognized by her manner of dress as belonging to a certain denomination. As she shared her agony and emotional pain, I moaned inwardly. I took her in my arms, encouraging her to go to her pastor for counseling. Her answer grieved me. She had been told by both her husband and her pastor that the beatings were because of her "rebellious nature."

"I don't know what else I can do to stop the abuse," she confided. "I've tried to please my husband. Scripturally, I cannot leave him. What can I do but stay with him? I don't want to disobey God, but I want the abuse to stop."

When we turn to the Scriptures, we find that God is much more merciful than we human beings. Jesus is our Example, and in one incident He turned around and walked away from the crowd who would have thrown Him off a cliff. (Luke 4:28-30.) There are times to take action; change brings change. Often, we want God to do something when all the time He is waiting for us to do something: **Trust God from the bottom of your heart; don't try to figure out everything on your own. Listen for God's voice in everything you do, everywhere you go; he's the one who will keep you on track** (Prov. 3:5,6 MESSAGE).

A testimony of deliverance from abusive behavior was shared by a young husband who had been born again for only a short time. His mother had given him a copy of *The Living Bible*. One day he picked it up and read Malachi 2:15-16: **You were united to your wife by the Lord. In God's wise plan, when you married, the two of you became one person in his sight. And what does he want? Godly children from your union. Therefore guard your passions! Keep faith with the wife of your youth. For the Lord, the God of Israel, says he hates divorce and cruel men. Therefore control your passions — let there be no divorcing of your wives.**

The young man said, "When I read these verses, I realized that I was treating my wife cruelly, and admitted to myself that the addictions in my life were controlling me. It wasn't so much that I wanted to stop doing drugs, but I did want to change the way that I was treating my wife. I cried out to God, and He heard me and delivered me."

The following prayer was written for Christian women who want to know how to pray prayers that avail much while in an abusive family situation.

Prayer

Father, Your Word says that You loved me and my family so much that You sent Your very own Son, Jesus, to die for our sin so we could live with You forever. You said that You would give us a new life that is wonderful and rich. I pray that I may become like You, for I am Your child and You love me.

By Your grace, Father, I will live my life in love. Your love in me is not a feeling, but a decision requiring more than mere words. As a Christian I am "light," and I will live as a child of the light. The light produces in me all that is good and right and true.

Lord, lead me in paths of righteousness for Your name's sake. I purpose to live, with a due sense of responsibility, not as others who do not know the meaning of life but as one who does. Direct me by Your Holy Spirit that I may make the best use of my time, despite all the evils of these days.

Father, there was a time that You looked for an intercessor. I am willing to stand in the gap and make up the hedge so that my family will not suffer judgment. Send Your Holy Spirit to convict, convince, and demonstrate to us about sin, righteousness, and judgment. Give us a heart of flesh, and send a laborer of the harvest to share with us the Gospel of the glory of Christ (the Messiah).

I thank You, Father, that each family member who is lost receives and confesses that Jesus is his/her Lord, and I ask that Your will be done in his/her life. It is You Who rescue him/her from the dominion of darkness, and You translate him/her into the Kingdom of the Son of Your love. In the name of Jesus, I ask that You help him/her to grow in grace that he/she may experience Your love and trust You to be his/her Father.

Lord, reveal the steps that I should take to break what appears to be a generational curse. The sins of the fathers are being repeated in our household, and I do not want this curse passed down to my children.

Father, Your Word says that we are overcomers by the blood of the Lamb, and by the word of our testimony. In the name of Jesus, I am committing my life to You — to obey You. Show me the path of life for me and my family.

Uncontrollable, irrational anger, rage, and abuse are a curse. Your Son Jesus was made a curse for us;

therefore, I put on Your whole armor that I may be able to successfully stand against all the strategies and the deceits of the devil.

In the name of Jesus, I am the redeemed, and I plead the blood of Jesus over my family. I thank You that the evil power of abuse is broken, overthrown, and cast down out of my family. The abuse is exposed and reproved by the light, it is made visible and clear; and where everything is visible and clear there is light.

You sent Jesus to bind up our heartaches and to heal our pain. The Bible says that You have sent Your Word to heal us and to deliver us from our own destructions. Give us the grace and faith to receive healing and to forgive those who have abused us; and thank You for the courage to make amends to those whom we have harmed.

Teach us how to guard our hearts with all diligence. I declare and decree that we are growing in grace and the knowledge of You, developing the trust we need to receive Your transforming power to change. I make my petitions known to You with thanksgiving, in the name of Jesus. Amen.

and humble in heart, and I will find rest for my soul. Your yoke is easy, and Your burden is light.

I look to You, Lord, and Your strength; I seek Your face always. You are my Refuge and Strength, an ever-present help in trouble. O my Strength, I watch for You; You, O God, are my Fortress, my loving God. O my Strength, I sing praise to You.

Father, You give strength to the weary and increase the power of the weak. Even youths grow tired and weary, and young men stumble and fall; but those who hope in You, Lord, will renew their strength. They will soar on wings like eagles; they will run and not grow weary. They will walk and not be faint. I purpose to wait for You, Lord; to be strong and take heart and wait for You.

Lord, You are my Strength and my Song; You have become my Salvation. You are my God, and I will praise You, my father's God, and I will exalt You. In Your unfailing love You will lead the people You have redeemed. In Your strength You will guide them to Your holy dwelling.

You, Sovereign Lord, have given me an instructed tongue, to know the word that sustains the weary. You waken me morning by morning, waken my ear to listen like one being taught.

You are my Light and my Salvation — whom shall I fear or dread? You are the Refuge and Stronghold of my life — of whom shall I be afraid? You are a Shield for me, my Glory, and the Lifter of my head. With my voice I cry to You, Lord, and You hear and answer me out of Your holy hill. Lord, You sustain me.

I consider it wholly joyful, whenever I am enveloped in or encounter trials of any sort or fall into various temptations. I am assured and understand that the trial and proving of my faith bring out endurance and steadfastness and patience. I purpose to let endurance and steadfastness and patience have full play and do a thorough work, so that I may be perfectly and fully developed [with no defects], lacking in nothing. I will praise You with my whole heart; Your joy is my strength.

I determine to consider Him Who endured such opposition from sinful men, so that I will not grow weary and lose heart.

Father, Your grace is sufficient, and I will not grow weary in doing good, for at the proper time I will reap a harvest if I do not give up. I am strong in You, Lord, and in Your mighty power.

In the name of Jesus I pray, amen.[1]

Scripture References

Psalm 119:28 NIV	Psalm 27:1 AMP
Matthew 11:28-30 NIV	Psalm 3:3,4 AMP
1 Chronicles 16:11 NIV	James 1:2-4 AMP
Psalm 46:1 NIV	Psalm 9:1
Psalm 59:9,17 NIV	Nehemiah 8:10
Isaiah 40:29-31 NIV	Hebrews 12:3 NIV
Psalm 27:14 NIV	2 Corinthians 12:9
Exodus 15:2,13 NIV	Galatians 6:9 NIV
Isaiah 50:4 NIV	Ephesians 6:10 NIV

---

[1] For additional strength and guidance I suggest reading and meditating on the following passages: Psalm 6, Psalm 18, Psalm 27, Psalm 28, Psalm 38, Psalm 71.

Dealing With a Child With ADD/ADHD

Introduction

In these last days Satan is working harder than ever to destroy our children. One of the areas of his attack is what psychologists and educators call Attention Deficit Disorder/Attention Deficit Hyperactivity Disorder. These disorders are tools of the enemy to disrupt households — causing confusion, frustration, division, and every evil work. Their effects are far reaching.

Children and adults with ADD/ADHD are thought of as bullies, unruly, destructive, overbearing, impulsive, defiant — and the list goes on. It has been estimated that about two to five percent of school-aged children are now diagnosed with the disorder, and many adults who have it have never been diagnosed. Many who might be helped if properly diagnosed are in mental institutions, jails, and prisons.[1]

---

[1] For additional information on ADD/ADHD including instructional practices for use in dealing with this disorder, see "101 WAYS TO HELP CHILDREN WITH ADD LEARN, Tips from Successful Teachers," published by Division of Innovation and Development, Office of Special Education Programs, Office of Special Education and Rehabilitative Services, U.S. Department of Education.

Although working with children diagnosed with ADD/ADHD can sometimes be frustrating and discouraging, as believers we know that God's Word, prayer, understanding caretakers, Christian counseling, medication, and their peers can all help them become overcomers.

In our ministry to these special children, we must remember that, according to 2 Corinthians 10:4, ...**the weapons of our warfare are not carnal, but mighty through God to the pulling down of strong holds.** Psalm 107:20 AMP says of the Lord's intervention on behalf of those in need, **He sends forth His word and heals them and rescues them from the pit and destruction.** Prayer, according to the Word of God, will avail much. (James 5:16.)

Declare and decree victory for the child as you teach and direct him/her through the following prayers.

The first two were written by a grandmother, one of our associates at Word Ministries, whose grandson has been diagnosed with ADD/ADHD. They pray together each morning before he leaves for school.

The third prayer and the following series of daily prayers were based on conversations and prayer times which I have had with this young man. He and I have cried and laughed together in my offices where we talk "privately" and confidentially.

At times, he asks to sit in a class where I am teaching, and later we discuss the subject matter. For instance, we may talk about abandonment issues, and how Jesus felt when He was on the cross. He is not shy about asking for prayer when he is having a problem.

If you use any of these prayers, I encourage you when necessary to explain in simple language the meaning of the terms found in them. Remember, the child's imagination is creating pictures with the words he or she speaks and hears.

As the child prays, listen carefully, allowing him/her to express his/her feelings, fears, thoughts, and ideas. Ask the Holy Spirit for discernment — it can be difficult to separate seriousness from horseplay. If you give the child time, he/she will let you know the difference.

Prayers To Be Prayed by the Child

I.

Coming Against ADD/ADHD

Father, in the name of Jesus, I come against ADD/ADHD and say that I have the mind of Christ (the Messiah) and hold the thoughts (feelings and purposes) of His heart; I am able to concentrate and stay focused on each task.

I am a disciple (taught by You, Lord, and obedient to Your will), and great is my peace and undisturbed composure. I do not have a spirit of fear, but [You have given me a spirit] of power and of love and of a calm, well-balanced mind and discipline and self-control.

In the name of Jesus, I come against my defiant behavior and tantrums and hyperactivity and speak peace and love to the situations in which I find myself. I cast down imaginations and every high thing that would exalt itself against the knowledge of You, Lord, and bring into captivity every thought to the obedience of Christ.

Father, I ask for Your wisdom to reside in me each day as I learn new techniques for handling stressful incidents.

Father, Your Word says not to worry about anything but to pray and ask You for everything I need and to give thanks when I pray, and Your peace will keep my heart and mind in Christ Jesus. The peace You give me is so great that I cannot understand it.

Thank You for keeping my mind quiet and at peace. I declare that I am an overcomer, I am in control.

In the name of Jesus, amen.

Scripture References

1 Corinthians 2:16 AMP	Philippians 4:6,7 ICB
Isaiah 54:13 AMP	Isaiah 26:3
2 Timothy 1:7 AMP	Revelation 12:11
2 Corinthians 10:5	

Tuesday:

Father, Psalm 91 says that You have assigned angels to me — giving them [especial] charge over me to accompany and defend and preserve me in all my ways.

Lord, I need Your help. Sometimes, my weird thoughts scare me, and I don't like the way I behave. I become so frightened and confused that I have to do something: run, make noises — even scream or try to hurt someone. These actions separate me from playmates, and when they don't want to be my friends, I am hurt and disappointed and angry.

I am asking You, Father, to help me form new behavior patterns and successfully overcome the disobedience and defiance that cause my parents and teachers anguish. I don't like to see them all upset, even though I laugh about it sometimes.

Thank You for helping me overcome obsessive, compulsive actions that create confusion for me and others around me. Even when others don't want me around, You will never abandon me. You will always be with me to help me and give me support.

In the name of Jesus, amen.

Scripture References

Psalm 91:11 AMP   Psalm 27:10 TLB
Romans 7:21-25 TLB   Hebrews 13:5 AMP

Wednesday:

Father, thank You for my parents, grandparents, wise counselors, and teachers who understand me and are helping me learn good behavior patterns. Help me to listen and develop good relationships with others — especially other children.

Thank You for giving me the ability to learn how to express my anger appropriately; I rejoice every time I have a victory. Your Son Jesus said that He has given me power to overcome all the obstacles that ADD/ADHD causes in my life.

In His name I pray, amen.

Scripture References

Ephesians 4:26 TLB   Luke 10:19 NIV

Thursday:

Father, I believe in my heart that Your Son Jesus is my Lord and Master, and that He has come to live in my heart. Thank You for giving me the mind of Christ (the Messiah), His thoughts (feelings and purposes).

Lord, You are with me when my thoughts get jumbled up, and You have sent the Holy Spirit to help me concentrate and stay focused on each task at home and at school. I am a disciple [taught by You, Lord, and obedient to Your will], and great is my peace and undisturbed composure. Thank You for giving me Your helmet of salvation to protect my thought life.

In the name of Jesus, amen.

Scripture References

Romans 10:9,10 NIV   Isaiah 54:13 AMP

1 Corinthians 2:16 AMP   1 Thessalonians 5:8 NIV
John 16:13 NIV

Friday:

Father, You have not given me a spirit of fear, but
You have given me a spirit of power and of love and a
calm, well-balanced mind and discipline and self-
control. Thank You that, as I grow in the grace and
knowledge of Jesus Christ, You are creating in me a
willing heart to be obedient.

Forgive me for throwing tantrums, and help me
recognize and control the destructive ideas that cause
them. The Holy Spirit is my Helper. Thank You for
giving me the ability to channel hyperactivity in
constructive, productive ways.

I choose to speak peace and love into the situations
that confront me and make me feel uncomfortable and
out of control.

In the name of Jesus, amen.

Scripture References

2 Timothy 1:7 AMP	Philippians 2:13
2 Peter 3:18	John 14:16 AMP
Exodus 35:5	

Saturday:

Father, sometimes awful thoughts come to me, and I command the voices that tell me bad things to be quiet and leave me in the name of Jesus.

Lord, in Your Word You said that I can make choices. I choose to cast down imaginations that cause me to feel afraid and angry; these thoughts are not Your thoughts. You love me, and I will think on good things.

Father, I ask for Your wisdom to reside in me each day as I learn new techniques for handling stressful incidents.

In the name of Jesus, amen.

Scripture References

Deuteronomy 30:19,20 TLB	Isaiah 55:8 TLB
2 Corinthians 10:5	Philippians 4:8 TLB

Sunday:

Father, there are so many everyday things that worry and torment me. I feel so different from other people.

Lord, Your Word says not to worry about anything but to pray and ask You for everything I need and to give thanks when I pray, and Your peace will keep my heart and mind in Christ Jesus. The peace You give me is so great that I cannot understand it.

Thank You for keeping my mind quiet and at peace. I declare that I am an overcomer, and by submitting to Your control, I am learning self-control.

Father, I thank You for teaching me how to be a good friend to those You are sending to be my friends.

In the name of Jesus, amen.

Scripture References

Philippians 4:6,7 ICB   Revelation 12:11

Isaiah 26:3 AMP   Galatians 5:23 AMP

Prayer To Be Prayed
By the Caregiver

Introduction

Caregivers of ADD/ADHD children often find themselves in situations that far exceed their parenting skills. Much prayer and faith are required to see the ADD/ADHD child as God sees him/her. The emotional turmoil and disruption to the household often become overwhelming and caregivers sometimes discover that the challenges are greater than themselves.

Responsible adults involved in the life of an ADD/ADHD child need godly wisdom, spiritual discernment, and mental and emotional alertness to overcome weariness, bewilderment, and anxiety. Often, they second guess themselves, processing confusing emotions and scenes of great conflict. Words spoken to the child and over him/her can comfort, giving him/her hope — or they can reinforce his/her belief that he/she is bad and that something terrible is wrong with him/her. Words can heal or words can wound.

The prayers of the ADD/ADHD child must be reinforced by those who love him/her. Often, our image of another individual — even our children — can only be changed as we pray according to God's will and purpose for him/her. The following personal prayer for the caregiver is a composite of things the Holy Spirit has directed me to pray for my friend and associate and her husband who are raising their ADD/ADHD grandson. I have observed in them the heartache, the delight, the exasperation — the full gamut of emotions involved in this challenging experience. But through it all, God is faithful!

Prayer

Father, in the name of Jesus, I thank You for this very special child. You see my confusion, anxiety, frustration, and bewilderment as I attempt to rear him/her [tenderly] in the training and discipline and the counsel and admonition of the Lord. Forgive me for times when I knowingly or unknowingly irritate and provoke him/her to anger [exasperate him/her to resentment].

You see my intense pain when I observe the rejection this child suffers by adults who speak harsh words against him/her and our family. Children refuse to play with him/her, and it hurts even though I understand. I know that those who have never walked in our shoes cannot fully understand us.

But, Lord, where others are unmerciful and unkind, You are merciful and kind. Surely, goodness and mercy shall follow us all the days of our lives, and we shall dwell in Your house forever. Hide us in the secret place of Your presence and keep us secretly in Your pavilion from the strife of tongues.

Lord, perfect the fruit of my lips that I may offer to You effective praise and thanksgiving for this child who is a blessing from You. His/her intellect astounds me, and his/her wit is a delight. I ask You for divine intervention and guidance as I train him/her up in the way that he/she should go. I thank You for the awesomeness of Your handiwork, and the techniques that You have given him/her to survive, to overcome emotional turmoil — and the ability to function in this world around us. Truly, this child is fearfully and wonderfully made. I plead the blood of Jesus over him/her to protect him/her in every situation.

You have a divine purpose for this child. You have foreordained steps that he/she is to walk in, works that he/she is to do. Help me to look at his/her strengths and weaknesses realistically, that I may know how to help him/her develop and demonstrate self-control techniques. Forgive me for times when I lose patience and berate him/her for his/her behavior. Sometimes, I lose sight of who he/she really is. Anoint my eyes to see him/her as You see him/her.

Father, help me to speak works of grace; anoint my lips to speak excellent and princely things over him/her, about him/her, and to him/her. May the opening of my lips be for right things. Help me to give him/her healthy doses of unconditional love, administer to him/her appropriate discipline for misbehavior, and reward him/her for his/her good behavior. Anoint my lips with coals of fire from Your altar that I may speak words that comfort, encourage, strengthen, and honor him/her. Keep watch at the door of my lips, and forgive me when my patience has come to an end.

Father, You are my Comforter, Counselor, Helper, Intercessor, Advocate, Strengthener, and Standby. Whatever comes my way, help me to consider it wholly joyful, allowing endurance and steadfastness and patience to have full play and do a thorough work, so that I may be perfectly and fully developed [with no defects], lacking in nothing. When I am deficient in wisdom, I will ask of You, and You will give wisdom to me liberally and ungrudgingly, without reproaching or finding fault in me.

I pray that I may be invigorated and strengthened with all power according to the might of Your glory, [to exercise] every kind of endurance and patience (perseverance and forbearance) with joy.

Father, You have seen the tears in the night season, and I know that I shall experience the joy that comes in the morning times. You are my Exceeding Joy! You are my wisdom, righteousness, sanctification, and redemption. Thank You for being a constant Companion.

Lord, I see my child, _____, growing and becoming strong in spirit, increasing in wisdom (in broad and full understanding) and in stature and years, and in favor with You and with man.

In the name of Jesus I pray, amen.

Scripture References

Ephesians 6:4 AMP	Isaiah 6:6,7
Psalm 117:2	Psalm 141:3 AMP
Psalm 23:6	John 14:16 AMP
Psalm 31:20 AMP	James 1:2,4,5 AMP
Hebrews 13:15	Colossians 1:11 AMP
Psalm 127:3 AMP	Psalm 22:2
Proverbs 22:6	Psalm 30:5
Psalm 139:14	Psalm 43:4
Ephesians 2:10	1 Corinthians 1:30
Proverbs 8:6 AMP	Luke 1:80; 2:52 AMP

Daily Affirmations for Use By the Caregiver

Introduction

Often it is very difficult for ADD/ADHD children to learn, to develop new learning techniques in their lives, and to change their negative behavior patterns. When working with them, it is so important that we love them with the God-kind of love and praise them for their accomplishments.

Following are examples of the kinds of positive daily affirmations that can be made to the ADD/ADHD child to help him/her develop a good self-image and to become all that God intends for him/her in this life.

Affirmations

• Great job • Well done • I'm very proud of you • Good for you • Neat • Outstanding • That was a smart decision • You are smart • God loves you • I love you • I knew you could do it • I believe in you • I know you are trying • Super-duper • You are a good boy/girl • Way to go • What an imagination • You are growing up • Good memory • Amazing • Nice work • What a wise choice • You are a blessing to me • You are special to me • You are valuable • You are a gem, a precious jewel • You are more precious than gold • You are incredible • You are important • Outstanding performance • You are a winner • Remarkable • Nothing can stop you • Now you've got it • Excellent • You are catching on • Great • Wonderful • Good • Terrific • Beautiful • Now you are cooking • You are fantastic • Beautiful work • Outstanding • You are spectacular • You are a real trooper • You are unique • Great discovery • You try so hard • Good try • Good effort • Magnificent • You've got it • Super work • Phenomenal • Marvelous • Dynamite • You mean so much to me • You make me laugh • You brighten my day • Hurray for you • You are beautiful • You are handsome • You are a good friend • You are a loving son/daughter [grandson/granddaughter] • You light up my life • You belong • You are an important part of our family • We are family • You mean the world to me • That's right • You are correct • You are a success • Hurray • You are growing in wisdom every day • You are a beautiful creation • You are loved • I love you • WOW! • You are a success • You are an overcomer • You are a child of my love • You are victorious • You are a ray of sunshine • You are patient • You have a good attitude • You are a doer • You know how to get the job done • You are a chosen one • You give good hugs • Thank you for being a part of my life•

You are deserving of praise!

Scripture Passages for Meditation

A GOOD REPORT: Proverbs 15:30; Philippians 4:8

A SOFT ANSWER: Proverbs 15:1

PERFECT LOVE: 1 John 4:18

Group
Prayers

part
two

Individual Growth

Father, in the name of Jesus, we in our prayer group desire that our prayers avail much. We are individuals who are [mutually dependent on one another], having gifts (faculties, talents, qualities) that differ according to the grace given us. We, who with unveiled faces all reflect Your glory, are being transformed into Your like- ness with ever-increasing glory, which comes from You, Who are the Spirit.

Father, we realize that You know what we have need of before we ask and that we are not all growing in the same manner or on the same time schedule, but we are growing in the grace and knowledge of our Lord and Savior Jesus Christ.

We give each other space to grow, for we are becoming a patient people, bearing with one another and making allowances because we love one another. We acknowledge that we do not have dominion [over] each other, and we refuse to lord it over one another's faith, but we are fellow laborers [to promote] one another's joy, because it is by faith that we stand firm.

In Jesus' name, amen.

Scripture References

James 5:16

Romans 12:5,6 AMP

2 Corinthians 3:18 NIV

Matthew 6:32

2 Peter 3:18

2 Corinthians 1:24 AMP

Ephesians 4:20

A Group Member Experiencing Grief or Loss

Father, in the name of Jesus, we approach Your throne of grace, bringing _____ before You. We recognize that grieving is a human emotional process, and we give him/her the space that he/she needs to enter into the rest that You have for him/her.

Lord, Jesus bore _____'s griefs (sicknesses, weaknesses, and distresses) and carried his/her sorrows and pains; we know that Your Spirit is upon Jesus to bind up and heal _____'s broken heart. May he/she be gentle with himself/herself, knowing that he/she is not alone in his/her grief. You are with him/her, and You will never leave him/her without support.

Give us, _____'s friends and prayer partners, discernment, sympathy, and understanding so that we may bear (endure, carry) his/her burden of loss. We trust You to guide him/her, and we respect his/her decisions awaiting the manifestation of Your healing.

Father, we desire to be doers of Your Word, and not hearers only. Therefore, we make a commitment to rejoice with those who rejoice [sharing others' joy], and to weep with those who weep [sharing others' grief]. We pray that our love will give _____ great joy and comfort and encouragement, because he/she has cheered and refreshed the hearts of Your people.

Thank You, Father, for sending the Holy Spirit to comfort, counsel, help, intercede, defend, strengthen, and stand by _____ in this time of grief and sorrow.

In Jesus' name, amen.

Scripture References

Isaiah 53:4 AMP   James 1:22

Isaiah 61:1 AMP   Romans 12:15 AMP

Hebrews 13:5 AMP   Philemon 7 AMP

Galatians 6:2 AMP   John 14:26 AMP

Loving and Caring for Self

Father, I realize that before I can love others as You have instructed, I must love myself. Help me to speak truly, deal truly, and live truly in harmony with You, myself, and others in my prayer group.

I am Your workmanship, created in Christ Jesus. I am fearfully and wonderfully made. Help me to remember that others do not always know what is best for me. I trust in You with all my heart and lean not on my own understanding; in all my ways I acknowledge You, and You will make my paths straight.

I look to You to cause my thoughts to be agreeable to Your will that I may make healthy choices. Give me the courage to say no when it is in my best interest according to Your purpose and plan for my life.

I take responsibility for myself and allow others in our prayer group to take responsibility for themselves, in the name of Jesus. This frees me so that I am not [merely] concerned with my own interests but also with the interests of others.

I desire to do unto others as I would have them do unto me. I am walking uprightly before You, therefore I consider, direct, and establish my way [with the confidence of integrity].

You are my confidence, and You will keep my foot from being snared. Your love is shed abroad in my heart, and I will love my neighbor as myself.

In Jesus' name, amen.

Scripture References

Romans 13:9	Philippians 2:4 AMP
Ephesians 4:15 AMP	Matthew 7:12
Ephesians 2:10	Proverbs 21:29 AMP
Psalm 139:14	Proverbs 3:26
Proverbs 3:5,6 NIV	Romans 5:5
Proverbs 16:3 AMP	Matthew 22:39

Perseverance in Prayer

Father, the course that You have set before me is clear. You have called me into this prayer group to respond to the many prayer requests we receive from those who need agreement or who don't know how to pray for themselves.

Lord, You are the Vinedresser; Jesus is the Vine; and I am the branch. I remain in Him and He remains in me, and my prayers bear much fruit; apart from Him, I can do nothing.

Father, at times I am tempted to grow weary and overburdened with the pain and heartache of others. Help me to remember that Jesus said, **"Come to me, all you who are weary and burdened, and I will give you rest"** (Matt. 11:28 NIV). I take His yoke upon me and learn from Him, for He is gentle and humble in heart, and I will find rest for my soul. His yoke is easy, and His burden is light.

Lord, Jesus said that I ought always to pray and not to turn coward (faint, lose heart, and give up). I am have their redemption through His blood, which means the remission of their sins.

Father, You delight at the sight of the Body of Christ, standing shoulder to shoulder in such orderly array and the firmness and the solid front and steadfastness of their faith in Christ, leaning on Him in absolute trust and confidence in His power, wisdom, and goodness. They walk — regulate their lives and conduct themselves — in union with and conformity to Him, having the roots of their being firmly and deeply planted in Him, being continually built up in Him, becoming increasingly more confirmed and established in the faith.

Your people, Father, clothe themselves as Your own picked representatives — Your chosen ones, who are purified and holy and well-beloved by You — by putting on behavior marked by tenderhearted pity and mercy, kind feeling, gentle ways, and patience. They have the power to endure whatever comes, with good temper. They are gentle and forbearing with each other and, if they have a grievance or complaint against another, readily pardon each other. As You, Lord, have freely forgiven them, so do they also forgive.

Your people put on love and enfold themselves with the bond of perfectness — which binds everything together completely in ideal harmony. They let the peace from Jesus act as umpire continually in their hearts — deciding and settling with all finality all the questions that arise in their minds — in that peaceful state to which they are called. They are thankful, appreciative, giving praise to You always.

The Body of Christ lets the Word spoken by Christ the Messiah have its home in their hearts and minds. It dwells in them in all richness, as they teach, admonish, and train each other in all insight, intelligence, and wisdom in spiritual songs, making melody to You, Father, with Your grace in their hearts.

And whatever they do in word or deed, they do everything in the name of the Lord Jesus and in dependence upon His person, giving praise to You, Father, through Him!

In Jesus' name, amen.

Scripture References (AMP)

Colossians 1:9-14   Colossians 2:5-7
Colossians 3:12-17

Unity and Harmony

Father, in the name of Jesus, this is the confidence that we have in You, that, if we ask anything according to Your will, You hear us: and since we know that You hear us, whatsoever we ask, we know that we have the petitions that we desire of You.

Father, You said, **Behold, they are one people, and they have all one language; and this is only the beginning of what they will do; and now nothing they have imagined they can do will be impossible to them** (Gen. 11:6 AMP). We pray by the name of our Lord Jesus, that all of us in Your Body be in perfect harmony, and full agreement in what we say, and that there be no dissensions or factions or divisions among us; but that we be perfectly united in our common understanding and in our opinions and judgments.

Holy Spirit, teach us how to agree (harmonize together, together make a symphony) about — anything

Vision for a Church

Father, in the name of Jesus, we come into Your presence thanking You for _____(name of church). You have called us to be saints in _____(name of city) and around the world. As we lift our voices in one accord, we recognize that You are God, and everything was made by and for You. We call into being those things that be not as though they were.

We thank You that we all speak the same thing: there is no division among us; we are perfectly joined together in the same mind. Grant unto us, Your representatives here, a boldness to speak Your Word which You will confirm with signs following. We thank You that we have workmen in abundance and all manner of cunning people for every manner of work. Each department operates in the excellence of ministry and intercessions. We have in our church the ministry gifts for the edifying of this body till we all come into the unity of the faith, and the knowledge of the Son of God, unto a mature person. None of our people will be children, tossed to and fro, and carried about with every wind of doctrine. We speak the truth in love.

We are a growing and witnessing body of believers becoming _____(number) strong. We have every need met. Therefore, we meet the needs of people who come — spirit, soul, and body. We ask for the wisdom of God in meeting these needs. Father, we thank You for the ministry facilities that will more than meet the needs of the ministry You have called us to. Our church is prospering financially, and we have more than enough to meet every situation. We have everything we need to carry out Your Great Commission and reach the _____(name of city or county) area for Jesus. We are a people of love as love is shed abroad in our hearts by the Holy Spirit. We thank You that the Word of God is living big in all of us and Jesus is Lord!

We are a supernatural church, composed of supernatural people doing supernatural things, for we are laborers together with God. We thank You for Your presence among us and we lift our hands and praise Your holy name! Amen.

Scripture References

Acts 4:24	Ephesians 4:11-15
Romans 4:17	Philippians 4:19
1 Corinthians 1:10	Romans 5:5
Acts 4:29	1 Corinthians 3:9
Mark 16:20b	Psalm 63:4
Exodus 35:33	

This prayer was written by and used with the permission of T. R. King; Valley Christian Center; Roanoke, Virginia.

Personal Prayer of a Pastor for the Congregation

Father, as the pastor of _____, I approach the throne of grace on behalf of the membership. I thank my God in all my remembrance of them. In every prayer of mine I always make my entreaty and petition for them all with joy (delight). [I thank my God] for their fellowship — their sympathetic co-operation and contributions and partnership — in advancing the good news (the Gospel). And I am convinced and sure of this very thing, that You have begun a good work in them and will continue until the day of Jesus Christ — right up to the time of His return — developing [that good work] and perfecting and bringing it to full completion in them.

In the name of Jesus, it is right and appropriate for me to have this confidence and feel this way about them all, because even as they do me, I hold them in my heart as partakers and sharers, one and all with me, of grace (God's unmerited favor and spiritual blessing).

be in the wrong. We pray that You prosper _____ abundantly, Lord — physically, spiritually, and financially.

We confess that _____ holds fast and follows the pattern of wholesome and sound teaching in all faith and love which is for us in Christ Jesus.

_____ guards and keeps with the greatest love the precious and excellently adapted Truth which has been entrusted to him/her by the Holy Spirit who makes His home in _____.

Lord, we pray and believe that, each and every day, freedom of utterance is given _____, that he/she will open his/her mouth boldly and courageously as he/she ought to do to get the Gospel to the people. Thank you, Lord, for the added strength which comes superhumanly that You have given him/her.

We hereby confess that we shall stand behind _____ and undergird him/her in prayer. We will say only that good thing that will edify _____. We will not allow ourselves to judge him/her, but will continue to intercede for him/her and speak and pray blessings upon him/her in the name of Jesus. Thank You, Jesus, for the answers. Hallelujah! Amen.

Scripture References

Isaiah 11:2,3	2 Timothy 1:13,14 AMP
Isaiah 61:1,6 AMP	Ephesians 6:19,20 AMP
Isaiah 54:17 AMP	1 Peter 3:12

Missionaries

Father, we lift before You those in the Body of Christ who are out in the field carrying the good news of the Gospel — not only in this country but also around the world. We lift those in the Body of Christ who are suffering persecution — those who are in prison for their beliefs. Father, we know that You watch over Your Word to perform it, that Your Word prospers in the thing for which You sent it. Therefore, we speak Your Word and establish Your covenant on this earth. We pray here and others receive the answer there by the Holy Spirit.

Thank You, Father, for revealing unto Your people the integrity of Your Word and that they must be firm in faith against the devil's onset, withstanding him. Father, You are their light, salvation, refuge, and stronghold. You hide them in Your shelter and set them high upon a rock. It is Your will that each one prospers, is in good health, and lives in victory. You set the prisoners free, feed the hungry, execute justice, rescue, and deliver.

In Jesus' name, we bind you, Satan, and every menacing spirit that would stir up against God's people.

We commission the ministering spirits to go forth and provide the necessary help for and assistance to these heirs of salvation. We and they are strong in the Lord and in the power of Your might, quenching every dart of the devil in Jesus' name.

Father, we use our faith covering these in the Body of Christ with Your Word. We say that no weapon formed against them shall prosper, and any tongue that rises against them in judgment they shall show to be in the wrong. This peace, security, and triumph over opposition is their inheritance as Your children. This is the righteousness which they obtain from You, Father, which You impart to them as their justification. They are far from even the thought of destruction, for they shall not fear and terror shall not come near them.

Father, You say You will establish them to the end — keep them steadfast, give them strength, and guarantee their vindication, that is, be their warrant against all accusation or indictment. They are not anxious beforehand how they shall reply in defense or what they are to say, for the Holy Spirit teaches them in that very hour and moment what they ought to say to those in the outside world, their speech being seasoned with salt.

We commit these our brothers and sisters in the Lord to You, Father, deposited into Your charge, entrusting them to Your protection and care, for You are faithful. You strengthen them and set them on a firm foundation and guard them from the evil one. We join our voices in praise unto You, Most High, that You might silence the enemy and avenger. Praise the Lord! Greater is He Who is in us than he who is in the world!

In His name we pray, amen.

Scripture References

Jeremiah 1:12	Ephesians 6:10,16
Isaiah 55:11	Isaiah 54:14,17
1 Peter 5:9	1 Corinthians 1:8
Psalm 27:1,5	Luke 12:11,12
3 John 2	Colossians 4:6
1 John 5:4,5	Acts 20:32
Psalm 146:7	2 Thessalonians 3:3
Psalm 144:7	Psalm 8:2
Matthew 18:18	1 John 4:4
Hebrews 1:14	

(making them to be fit, worthy and sufficient) as ministers and dispensers of a new covenant. They are not ministers of the law which kills, but of the (Holy) Spirit which makes alive.

Father, we rejoice in the Lord over our teachers and commit to undergird them with our faith and love. We will not judge or criticize them, but speak excellent and princely things concerning them. The opening of our lips shall be for right things.

Thank You, Father, that the teachers live in harmony, with the other members of our church, being in full accord and of one harmonious mind and intention. Each is not [merely] concerned for his/her own interests, but each for the interest of others. Jesus is our example in humility, and our teachers shall tend — nurture, guard, guide, and fold — the flock of God which is [their responsibility], and will be examples of Christian living to the flock (the congregation).

Thank You, Father, for the performance of Your Word in our midst, in the name of Jesus. Amen.

Scripture References (AMP)

Exodus 31:3,4	2 Corinthians 3:5b,6
Romans 12:7	Proverbs 8:6
James 3:1,2	Philippians 2:2,4,5
Ephesians 4:12-15	1 Peter 5:2,3
Philippians 2:13	Jeremiah 1:12

A Christian Counselor

Father, in the name of Jesus, I pray for _____ to exhort and counsel the emotionally wounded. I ask in faith that Your Spirit will rest upon him/her, the Spirit of wisdom and understanding, the Spirit of counsel and might. Give him/her insight and knowledge for understanding his/her counselees' responses to circumstances.

Thank You, Father, that _____ is a good listener to the confessions of his/her counselees. Help him/her to comprehend the unfolding of those past hurts which influence reactions to current situations.

Lord, _____ will not judge by what he/she sees with his/her eyes, or decide by what he/she hears with his/her ears. He/she will judge the needy and give decisions with justice. Righteousness will be his/her belt, and faithfulness the sash around his/her waist. He/she will be clothed with fairness and with truth.

Thank You that _____ is a promoter of peace and is filled with joy. Grant Your counselor, out of the rich treasury of Your glory, to be strengthened and reinforced with mighty power in the inner man by the [Holy] Spirit [Himself indwelling his/her innermost being and personality].

You will not leave _____ without support as he/she gives his/her time and concern, helping to complete the forgiveness process. He/she will be confident about his/her convictions, knowing excellent things, and will have the knowledge to assist Your children in knowing the certainty of the words of truth.

In Jesus' name, amen.

Scripture References

Isaiah 11:2,3   Ephesians 3:16 AMP
Isaiah 11:4,5 NIV   Proverbs 22:20,21 AMP
Isaiah 11:5 TLB

Prosperity for Ministering Servants

Father, how we praise You and thank You for Your Word, knowing that You watch over Your Word to perform it, and no Word of Yours returns void, but accomplishes that which You please, and it prospers in the thing for which You sent it.

Father, in the name of Jesus, we pray, confess and believe according to Your Word that those in Your Body who have sown the seed of spiritual good among the people reap from the people's material benefits, for You directed that those who publish the good news of the Gospel should live and get their maintenance by the Gospel.

We confess that Your ministers seek and are eager for the fruit which increases to the people's credit — the harvest of blessing that is accumulating to their account. The people's gifts are the fragrant odor of an offering and sacrifice which You, Father, welcome and in which You delight. You will liberally supply, fill to the full, the people's every need according to Your riches in glory in Christ Jesus.

We confess that those then who receive instruction in the Word of God share all good things with their teachers, contributing to their support. We confess that Your people will not lose heart and grow weary and faint in acting nobly and doing right, for in due time and at the appointed season they shall reap, if they do not loosen and relax their courage and faint.

So then, as occasion and opportunity are open to the people, they do good to all people not only being useful and profitable to them, but also doing what is for their spiritual good and advantage.

We confess that Your people are a blessing, especially to those of the household of faith — those who belong to God's family, the believers. Thus, we believe and confess Your people sow generously that blessings may come to someone. Your people then reap generously and with blessings, for You love, take pleasure in, prize above other things, and are unwilling to abandon or do without a cheerful, joyous, prompt-to-do-it giver whose heart is in his giving.

God, You are then able to make all grace, every favor and earthly blessing, come to Your people in abundance, so that they are always and under all circumstances possessing enough to require no aid or support and furnished in abundance for every good work and charitable donation.

As Your people give, their deeds of justice and goodness and kindness and benevolence go on and endure forever. And God, You provide the seed for the sower and bread for the eating, so You also will provide and multiply the people's resources for sowing and increase the fruits of their righteousness. Thus Your people are enriched in all things and in every way so that they can be generous, and their generosity, as it is administered by Your teachers, will bring thanksgiving to God.

As it is written, **Give, and it shall be given unto you; good measure, pressed down, and shaken together,**

and running over, shall men give into your bosom
(Luke 6:38). Praise the Lord!

In Jesus' name, amen.

Scripture References

Jeremiah 1:12	Galatians 6:6-10
Isaiah 55:11	2 Corinthians 9:6-11
1 Corinthians 9:11-14	Luke 6:38
Philippians 4:17-19	

A Ministry in Need of Finances

Introduction

This prayer was written in response to an appeal for help from a ministry in a financial crunch. This ministry reaches out to people addicted to drugs, alcohol, and other substances, and then out beyond the youths and adults to their families. After we had prayed the following prayer, it was given to our editor and prayer request correspondent. It can be used to pray for the needs of any ministry.

Prayer

Father, in the name of Jesus, we believe that all of the needs of _____ are met, according to Philippians 4:19. We believe that because this ministry has given tithes and offerings to further Your cause to help youth, adults, and families come to the knowledge of the truth, [gifts] will be given to them, good measure; pressed down, shaken together, and running over will they be poured into their bosom. For with the measure they deal out, it will be measured back to them.

Father, in the name of Jesus, we pray, confess, and believe according to Your Word that those in Your Body who have sown [the seed of] spiritual good among the people will reap from the people's material benefits, for You have directed that those who publish the good news of the Gospel should live and get their maintenance by the Gospel.

We confess that Your ministers with _____ Ministry seek and are eager for the fruit which increases to the people's credit [the harvest of blessing that is accumulating to their account]. The people's gifts are the fragrant odor of an offering and sacrifice which You, Father, welcome and in which You delight. You will liberally supply (fill to the full) the people's every need according to Your riches in glory in Christ Jesus.

Father, we call forth partners who will respond to Your call to support this ministry, prayerfully and financially.

Lord, we thank You for directing the leader, _____, who seeks Your ways, teaching him/her the fortitude of Your Word and the steadfastness of its

PRAYERS THAT AVAIL MUCH COMMEMORATIVE GIFT EDITION

truth. Your anointing which destroys the yoke of
bondage abides within him/her permanently. Teach
him/her to pray for the people and the government of
our land. We thank You for Your Word which brings
freedom to the hearers, and we thank You for preparing
their hearts to receive the good news of the Gospel.

Lord, strengthen (complete, perfect) and make
_____ what he/she ought to be, equipping him/her
with everything good that he/she may carry out Your
will; [while You Yourself] work in him/her and accomplish that which is pleasing in Your sight, through Jesus
Christ (the Messiah); to Whom be the glory forever
and ever (to the ages of the ages).

In His name we pray, amen.

Scripture References

Luke 6:38 AMP	Isaiah 10:27
1 Corinthians 9:11,13 AMP	1 Timothy 2:1-3 AMP
Philippians 4:17-19 AMP	John 8:32
Matthew 9:38 AMP	Hebrews 13:21 AMP

tual understanding, that he/she may walk worthy of You, Lord, being fruitful in every good work and increasing in the knowledge of You. _____ is merciful, as his/her Father is merciful. Because he/she doesn't judge other people, he/she will not be judged. He/she does not condemn and he/she will not be condemned.

_____ forgives others and people forgive him/her. _____ gives and men will give to him/her — yes, good measure, pressed down, shaken together, and running over will they pour into his/her lap. For whatever measure he/she uses with other people, they will use in their dealings with him/her.

In Jesus' name we pray, amen.

Scripture References

Galatians 5:22,23   Psalm 1:3

Galatians 2:20   Colossians 1:9

Mark 4:8   Luke 6:36-38 PHILLIPS

II.

Father, it is our prayer that good will come to
_____. He/she is generous and lends freely. He/she
conducts his/her affairs with justice.

Lord, Your Word says that surely _____ will
never be shaken. He/she is a righteous man/woman
who will be remembered forever. He/she will have no
fear of bad news; his/her heart is steadfast, trusting in
You, Lord.

_____'s heart is secure, he/she will have no fear;
in the end he/she will look in triumph on his/her foes.
He/she has scattered abroad his/her gifts to the poor,
his/her righteousness endures forever; his/her horn will
be lifted high in honor.

We pray that Your plans will be fulfilled in
_____'s life, and we thank You for Your mercies on
his/her behalf.

In the name of Jesus, amen.

Scripture References

Psalm 112:5-9 NIV   Jeremiah 29:11 NIV

Overcoming Prejudice

Introduction

The previous few days in Miami had been exceptionally cool. Jan, my traveling companion, and I did not consider it coat weather, but the Floridians shivered, all bundled up in their winter wear.

The prayer seminar had gone well, and it was now our last service before leaving for home. The preparation for the Sunday morning worship service had been difficult, and I found myself at the mercy of the Holy Spirit. (Not a bad place to be!)

During the preliminaries and the praise and worship service, I was crying out inwardly, just for a starting Scripture that I could read.

The sanctuary was packed as I stood before the congregation of beautiful skin tones — from almost white to light chocolate to black velvet. Their faces looked back at me. I smiled and began to read a psalm — making comments as I felt prompted by the Holy Spirit.

Where is the *flow* of the Spirit? I wondered. God, what is it You want to do in this church today?

The tension within me grew, and I felt helpless.

At last, I knew. (Sometimes, it is good that we do not know what we will say beforehand. We might mess it all up, working to be politically correct, writing and rewriting to make sure that we cross every "t" and dot every "i" with the correct flourish.)

The love of God began to rise within me. I spoke from my heart of hearts:

"You cannot really know me unless I choose to share myself — my thoughts, my ideas, and my feelings. Obviously, I am a Southern white woman. I grew up in cotton mill towns in North Georgia. There I attended the all-white Pentecostal churches where my dad served as pastor. I attended all-white schools and lived in all-white neighborhoods. The only black people I knew were Smut and Clarabell, tenants on my uncle's farm.

"I don't know if I have any racial prejudice — it has never been tested. I know that at one time I was filled with intellectual prejudice, because God exposed it in a very dramatic way. If I have any racial prejudice, I want the Holy Spirit to uncover it and deliver me. All I know is that I love you, and we are one — one blood. In Christ Jesus there is neither Jew nor Greek, male nor female, black nor white. There is that one new man created in Him."

The barriers came tumbling down. My newly found friends, brothers and sisters in the Lord, no longer hugged from a distance. Many smothered me in bear hugs after the benediction. The unity of the Spirit had prevailed. (Eph. 4:3.)

Jesus is our peace, and I believe that the Scriptures written by the Apostle Paul in Galatians and Ephesians apply today.

Ethnic groups are assuming responsibility for the sins of the forefathers, and asking forgiveness for past wrongs done to one another. We are accountable to God and each other as members of one household, and by the blood of the Lamb and through good communication we are overcoming the dividing schemes of the devil. God is bringing His people together. Red and yellow, black and white — we are coming together — and we are precious in His sight.

We are no longer outsiders or aliens, but fellow-citizens with every other Christian — we belong now to the household of God. (Eph. 2:19 PHILLIPS.)

Prayer

Father, in the name of Jesus, we come before You, asking Your forgiveness for being intolerant of one another because of the color of our skin. Forgive us for tolerating prejudice in the household of faith. Set us free from the influence of public opinion that we may live out our glorious, Christ-originated faith.

Forgive us for segregating ourselves by color, by a measure of wealth or intellect. We are all Your children, the sheep of Your pasture. You made us, and not we ourselves.

We are one blood, redeemed by the blood of the Lamb, Who was slain before the foundation of the world. We are baptized "into" Christ and have put on the family likeness of Christ.

We call for an end to division and segregation in Christ's family — may there be no division into Jew and non-Jew, slave and free, male and female. Among us we are all equal. That is, we are all in a common relationship with Jesus Christ.

Thank You, Father, for bringing us together in Christ through His death on the cross. The cross got us to embrace, and that was the end of the hostility.

Lord, Jesus came and preached peace to us outsiders and peace to us insiders. He treated us as equals, and so made us equals. Through Him we share the same Spirit and have equal access to You, Father.

The Kingdom of faith is now our home country, and we are no longer strangers or outsiders. We *belong* here.

Lord, You are building a home. You are using us all — irrespective of how we got here — in what You are building. You are fitting us in with Christ Jesus as the cornerstone Who holds all the parts together. We see it taking shape day after day — a holy temple built by You, Father, all of us built into it, a temple in which You are quite at home.

Father, You have called us all to travel on the same road and in the same direction, so we will stay together, both outwardly and inwardly. We have one Master, one faith, one baptism, one God and Father of all, Who rules over all, works through all, and is present in all. Everything we are and think and do is permeated with oneness.

Father, we imitate You. We walk in love, [esteeming and delighting in one another]. We walk as children of the light [leading the lives of those native-born to the light]. We look carefully how we walk! We live purpose-fully and worthily and accurately, making the very most of the time [buying up each opportunity], because the days are evil.

We speak out to one another in psalms and hymns and spiritual songs, offering praise with voice [and instruments] and making melody with all our hearts to You, Lord, at all times and for everything giving thanks in the name of our Lord Jesus Christ to You, Father. By love we serve one another.

Thank You, Father, that prejudice is being rooted out of the Body of Christ, in the name of Jesus. Amen.

Scripture References

James 2:1 MESSAGE

Psalm 100:3

1 Peter 1:18 NIV

Galatians 3:27 PHILLIPS

Galatians 3:28 MESSAGE

Ephesians 2:13-22 MESSAGE

Ephesians 4:3-6 MESSAGE

Ephesians 5:1,2,8 AMP

Ephesians 5:15,16,19,20 AMP

Galatians 5:13 AMP

Your assignments. You have called us by Your grace for such a time as this. We rejoice in the outpouring of Your Spirit on this ministry.

In the name of Jesus, amen.

Scripture References

Psalm 33:1	1 John 2:27
Psalm 118:24	1 Corinthians 6:20
1 Corinthians 12:3	Ephesians 5:1,2 AMP
Matthew 6:10	James 5:7
Colossians 1:13	1 Peter 5:10
Deuteronomy 30:19	Esther 4:14
Isaiah 10:27	Acts 2:17

Ministers to the Incarcerated

Introduction

This prayer was written in response to a letter from an inmate. He had received Jesus, started a Bible study, and wanted to know how to pray for God-called teachers and preachers to come and teach the inmates. He was praying for prisoners who did not know Jesus, believing that revival was coming to the correctional facility where he was housed.

Prayer

Father, You said that whoever calls upon the name of the Lord will be saved. How shall the inmates at this correctional facility/prison call on Him in Whom they have not believed? And how shall they believe in Him of Whom they have not heard? And how shall they hear without a preacher? And how shall they preach unless they are sent? We ask You, the Lord of the harvest, to send Your chosen laborers to preach deliverance to the captives of this prison.

Father, we thank You for Your ministers who are willing to go and preach deliverance to the incarcerated. May You grant to them out of the rich treasury of Your glory to be strengthened and reinforced with mighty power in the inner man by the [Holy] Spirit [Himself indwelling their innermost being and personality]. Anoint their lips to preach the good news of the Gospel.

Father, send Your Holy Spirit to go before the ministers, anoint the ears of the hearers, and prepare their hearts to hear, receive, love, and obey Your Word. Thank You that the light of the Gospel shines in their hearts so as to beam forth the light for the illumination of the knowledge of Your majesty and glory so that everyone who calls on Your name shall be saved.

Father, thank You for creating a desire within Your ministers to diligently study Your Word that they might show themselves approved unto You, workmen who will not be put to shame, rightly dividing Your Word of truth. They are living witnesses to those who are not yet obedient to the Gospel.

Father, we thank You for an outpouring of Your Spirit upon the staff and inmates of this facility. We know that faith comes by hearing, and hearing by Your Word. We thank You for the salvation and deliverance of all those who call upon Your name.

In the name of Jesus, we thank You for sending the Holy Spirit Who reveals truth to sinners, convicting and convincing them of sin, righteousness, and judgment.

We release Your mercy, Your love, and Your grace to those within these walls that they might be saved through faith, and that not of themselves; it is Your gift.

Thank You, Lord, for hearing our prayer on behalf of the people at this correctional facility/prison.

In Jesus' name, amen.

Scripture References

Romans 10:13,14	Romans 15:18
Matthew 9:38	Acts 2:18
Ephesians 3:16 AMP	Romans 10:17
2 Corinthians 4:6 AMP	John 16:8,13
Romans 10:13	Ephesians 2:8
2 Timothy 2:15	

Revival

Father, in the name of Jesus, You have revived us again that Your people may rejoice in You. Thank You for showing us Your mercy and lovingkindness, O Lord, and for granting us Your salvation. You have created in us a clean heart, O God, and renewed a right, persevering and steadfast spirit within us. You have restored unto us the joy of Your salvation, and You are upholding us with a willing spirit. Now we will teach transgressors Your ways, and sinners shall be converted and return to You.

We therefore cleanse our ways by taking heed and keeping watch [on ourselves] according to Your Word [conforming our lives to it]. Since Your [great] promises are ours, we cleanse ourselves from everything that contaminates and defiles our bodies and spirits, and bring [our] consecration to completeness in the (reverential) fear of God. With our whole hearts have we sought You, inquiring for You and of You, and yearning for You; O let us not wander or step aside [either in ignorance or willfully] from Your commandments. Your

Word have we laid up in our hearts, that we might not sin against You.

Jesus, thank You for cleansing us through the Word — the teachings — which You have given us. We delight ourselves in Your statutes; we will not forget Your Word. Deal bountifully with Your servants, that we may live; and we will observe Your Word [hearing, receiving, loving, and obeying it].

Father, in the name of Jesus, we are doers of the Word, and not merely listeners to it. It is You, O Most High, Who has revived and stimulated us according to Your Word! Thank You for turning away our eyes from beholding vanity [idols and idolatry]; and restoring us to vigorous life and health in Your ways. Behold, we long for Your precepts; in Your righteousness give us renewed life. This is our comfort and consolation in our affliction, that Your Word has revived us and given us life.

We strip ourselves of our former natures — put off and discard our old unrenewed selves — which characterized our previous manner of life. We are constantly renewed in the spirit of our minds — having a fresh mental and spiritual attitude; and we put on the new nature (the regenerate self) created in God's image, (Godlike) in true righteousness and holiness. Though our outer man is (progressively) decaying and wasting away, our inner self is being (progressively) renewed day after day. Hallelujah! Amen.

Scripture References (AMP)

Psalm 85:6,7	James 1:22
Psalm 51:10,12,13	Psalm 119:25
Psalm 119:9-11	Psalm 119:37,40,50
2 Corinthians 7:1	Ephesians 4:22-24
John 15:3	2 Corinthians 4:16b
Psalm 119:16,17	

Success of a Meeting

Father, in the name of Jesus, we openly confess that the Word of God will come forth boldly and accurately during the _____(meeting) and that the people who hear Your Word will not be able to resist the wisdom and the inspiration of the Holy Spirit that will be spoken through Your minister(s) of the Gospel.

We confess that, as Your Word comes forth, an anointing of the Holy Spirit will cause people to open their spiritual eyes and ears and turn from darkness to light — from the power of Satan to You, God, and make Jesus their Lord.

We commit this meeting to You, Father, we deposit it into Your charge — entrusting this meeting, the people who will hear, and the people who will speak into Your protection and care. We commend this meeting to the Word — the commands and counsels and promises of Your unmerited favor. Father, we know Your Word will build up the people and cause them to realize that they are joint-heirs with Jesus.

We believe, Father, that as Your Word comes forth, an anointing will be upon the speaker and _____(name) will be submitted completely to the Holy Spirit, for the Word of God that is spoken is alive and full of power, making it active, operative, energizing, and effective, being sharper than any two-edged sword. We believe that every need of every person will be met spiritually, physically, mentally, and financially.

We thank You, Father, and praise You that, because we have asked and agreed together, these petitions have come to pass. Let these words with which we have made supplication before the Lord be near to the Lord our God day and night, that He may maintain the cause and right of His people in the _____(meeting) as each day of it requires! We believe that all the earth's people will know that the Lord is God and there is no other! Hallelujah! Amen.

Scripture References (AMP)

James 5:16	Acts 26:18
Matthew 18:19	Acts 20:32

Ephesians 6:19	Hebrews 4:12
Acts 6:10	Philippians 4:19
Ephesians 1:18	1 Kings 8:59,60

Success of a Conference

Father, we pray that those who hear the messages at the _____ conference will believe — adhere to and trust in and rely on Jesus as the Christ, and that all those You have called to attend the conference will be there and receive what You have for them.

Let it be known and understood by all that it is in the name and through the power and authority of Jesus Christ of Nazareth, and by means of Him that this conference is successful.

The speakers shall be filled with and controlled by the Holy Spirit. When the people see the boldness and unfettered eloquence of the speakers, they shall marvel and recognize that they have been with Jesus. Everybody shall be praising and glorifying God for what shall be occuring. By the hands of the ministers, numerous and startling signs and wonders will be performed among the people.

Father, in the name of Jesus, we thank You that You have observed the enemy's threats and have granted us, Your bondservants, full freedom to declare Your message fearlessly — while You stretch out Your hand to cure and perform signs and wonders through the authority and by the power of the name of Your Holy Child and Servant Jesus.

We thank You, Father, that when we pray, the place in which we are assembled will be shaken; and we shall all be filled with the Holy Spirit, and Your people shall continue to speak the Word of God with freedom and boldness and courage.

By common consent, we shall all meet together at the conference. More and more individuals shall join themselves with us — a crowd of both men and women. The people shall gather from the north, south, east, and west, bringing the sick and those troubled with foul spirits, and they shall all be cured.

Thank You, Father, that our speakers are men and women of good and attested character and repute, full of the Holy Spirit and wisdom. The people who shall hear will not be able to resist the intelligence and the wisdom and the inspiration of the Spirit with which they speak, in the name of Jesus.

Thank You, Father, for the performance of Your Word in the name of Jesus! Amen.

Scripture References (AMP)

Acts 4:10,13,21	Acts 5:12b,13,16
Acts 5:12a	Acts 6:3,10
Acts 4:29-31	

Protection and Deliverance of a City

Father, in the name of Jesus, we have received Your power — ability, efficiency, and might — because the Holy Spirit has come upon us; and we are Your witnesses in _____ and to the ends — the very bounds — of the earth.

We fearlessly and confidently and boldly draw near to the throne of grace that we may receive mercy and find grace to help in good time for every need — appropriate help and well-timed help, coming just when we in the city of _____ need it.

Father, thank You for sending forth Your commandments to the earth; Your Word runs very swiftly throughout _____. Your Word continues to grow and spread.

Father, we seek — inquire for, require and request — the peace and welfare of _____ in which You have caused us to live. We pray to You for the welfare of this city and do our part by getting involved in it. We will not let [false] prophets and diviners who are in our midst deceive us; we pay no attention and attach no significance to our dreams which we dream, or to theirs. Destroy [their schemes], O Lord; confuse their tongues; for we have seen violence and strife in the city.

Holy Spirit, we ask You to visit our city and open the eyes of the people, that they may turn from darkness to light, and from the power of Satan to God, so that they may thus receive forgiveness and release from their sins and a place and portion among those who are consecrated and purified by faith in Jesus.

Father, we pray for deliverance and salvation for those who are following the course and fashion of this world — who are under the sway of the tendency of this present age — following the prince of the power of the air.

Father, forgive them, for they know not what they do.

We speak to the prince of the power of the air, to the god of this world who blinds the unbelievers' minds (that they should not discern the truth), and we command that he leave the heavens above our city.

Thank You, Father, for the guardian angels assigned to this place who war for us in the heavenlies.

In the name of Jesus, we stand victorious over the principalities, powers, rulers of the darkness of this world, and spiritual wickedness in high places over _____.

We ask the Holy Spirit to sweep through the gates of our city and convince the people and bring demonstration to them about sin and about righteousness — uprightness of heart and right standing with God — and about judgment.

Father, You said, **For I know the thoughts and plans that I have for you...thoughts and plans for welfare and peace, and not for evil, to give you hope in your final outcome** (Jer. 29:11 AMP). By the blessing of the influence of the upright and God's favor [because of them] the city of _____ is exalted. Amen.

Scripture References

Acts 1:8 AMP	Luke 23:34a AMP
Hebrews 4:16 AMP	2 Corinthians 4:4 AMP

Psalm 147:15 AMP   Ephesians 6:12
Acts 12:24 AMP   Psalm 101:8 AMP
Jeremiah 29:7,8 AMP   John 16:8 AMP
Psalm 55:9 AMP   Jeremiah 29:11 AMP
Acts 26:18 AMP   Proverbs 11:11a AMP
Ephesians 2:2 AMP

Protection From Terrorism

Father, in the name of Jesus, we praise You and offer up thanksgiving because the Lord is near — He is coming soon. Therefore, we will not fret or have any anxiety about the terrorism that is threatening the lives of those who travel and those stationed on foreign soil or at home. But in this circumstance and in everything by prayer and petition [definite requests] with thanksgiving we continue to make our wants known to You.

Father, our petition is that terrorism in the heavenlies and on earth be stopped before it spreads to other countries and comes to our land, _____.

Jesus, You have given us the authority and power to trample upon serpents and scorpions and (physical and mental strength and ability) over all the power that the enemy [possesses], and nothing shall in any way harm us.

Therefore, in the name of Jesus, we address and take authority over the prince of the power of the air and over the principalities, powers, the rulers of the darkness of this world, and spiritual wickedness in high places who have been assigned by Satan to terrorize God-fearing governments and their people.

Satan, we bind your works and render them null and void in the name of Jesus Christ of Nazareth, and we forbid you to operate in _____. We cast you out of our land and other God-fearing countries and command you to turn back in this day as we cry out; for this we know, that God is for us — and if God be for us who can be against us?

In the name of Jesus, we take authority over a spirit of timidity — of cowardice, of craven and cringing and fawning fear (of terrorism) — for [God has given us a spirit] of power and of love and of calm and well-balanced mind and discipline and self-control.

We shall not be afraid of the terror of the night, nor of the arrow [the evil plots and slanders of the wicked] that flies by day, nor of the pestilence that stalks in darkness, nor of the destruction and sudden death that surprise and lay waste at noonday.

Therefore, we establish ourselves on righteousness, rightness — [right], in conformity with God's will and order; we shall be far from even the thought of oppression or destruction, for we shall not fear; and from terror, for it shall not come near us.

Holy Spirit, thank You for writing this Word upon the tablets of our hearts so that we can speak it out of our mouths, for we will order our conversation aright and You will show us the salvation of God. Hallelujah! Amen.

Scripture References

Philippians 4:5,6b AMP   Romans 8:31b

Luke 10:19 AMP   2 Timothy 1:7 AMP

Ephesians 6:10 AMP   Psalm 91:5,6 AMP

Ephesians 2:2 AMP   Isaiah 54:14 AMP

Ephesians 6:12 AMP   Proverbs 3:3b AMP

Matthew 16:19   Psalm 50:23

Psalm 56:9 AMP

Salvation of the Lost

Father, it is written in Your Word, **First of all, then, I admonish and urge that petitions, prayers, intercessions and thanksgivings be offered on behalf of all men** (1 Timothy 2:1 AMP).

Therefore, Father, we bring the lost of the world this day — every man, woman, and child from here to the farthest corner of the earth — before You. As we intercede, we use our faith believing that thousands this day have the opportunity to make Jesus their Lord.

For everyone who has that opportunity, Satan, we bind your blinding spirit of antichrist and loose you from your assignment against those who have that opportunity to make Jesus Lord.

We ask the Lord of the harvest to thrust the perfect laborers across these lives this day to share the good news of the Gospel in a special way so that they will listen and understand it. We believe that they will not be able to resist the wooing of the Holy Spirit, for You, Father, bring them to repentance by Your goodness and love.

We confess that they shall see who have never been told of Jesus. They shall understand who have never heard of Jesus. And they shall come out of the snare of the devil who has held them captive. They shall open their eyes and turn from darkness to light — from the power of Satan to You, God!

In Jesus' name, amen.

Scripture References

1 Timothy 2:1,2 AMP	Romans 2:4
Matthew 18:18	Romans 15:21 AMP
Matthew 9:38	2 Timothy 2:26 AMP

Nations and Continents

Father, in the name of Jesus, we bring before You the nation (or continent) of _____ and its leaders. Father, You say in Your Word that you reprove leaders for our sakes so that we may live a quiet and peaceable life in all godliness and honesty.

We pray that skillful and godly wisdom has entered into the heart of _____'s leaders and that knowledge is pleasant to them, that discretion watches over them and understanding keeps them and delivers them from the way of evil and from the evil men.

We pray that the upright shall dwell in the government(s)...that men and women of integrity, blameless and complete in Your sight, Father, shall remain, but the wicked shall be cut off and the treacherous shall be rooted out. We pray that those in authority winnow the wicked from among the good and bring the threshing wheel over them to separate the chaff from the grain, for loving-kindness and mercy, truth and faithfulness preserve those in authority and their offices are upheld by the people's loyalty.

We confess and believe that the decisions made by the leaders are divinely directed by You, Father, and their mouths should not transgress in judgment. Therefore, the leaders are men and women of discernment, understanding and knowledge so the stability of _____ will long continue. We pray that the uncompromisingly righteous be in authority in _____ so that the people there can rejoice.

Father, it is an abomination for leaders to commit wickedness. We pray that their offices be established and made secure by righteousness and that right and just lips are a delight to those in authority and that they love those who speak what is right.

We pray and believe that the good news of the Gospel is published in this land. We thank You for laborers of the harvest to publish Your Word that Jesus is Lord in _____. We thank You for raising up intercessors to pray for _____ in Jesus' name. Amen.

Scripture References

1 Timothy 2:1,2	Proverbs 16:10,12,13 AMP
Psalm 105:14	Proverbs 28:2 AMP
Proverbs 2:10-15 AMP	Proverbs 29:2 AMP
Proverbs 2:21,22 AMP	Acts 12:24
Proverbs 20:26,28 AMP	Psalm 68:11
Proverbs 21:1	

* * *

Here is a list of continents and nations to help you as you pray for the world:

Continents:

Africa	North America
Asia	Oceania
Europe	South America

Nations:

Abkhazia	Angola
Afghanistan	Anguilla
Albania	Antigua and Barbuda
Algeria	Argentina
Andorra	Armenia

Aruba
Austria
Azerbaijan
Bahamas
Bahrain
Bangladesh
Barbados
Belarus
Belgium
Belize
Benin
Bermuda
Bhutan
Bolivia
Bosnia-Hercegovina
Botswana
Brazil
British Antartic Territory
British Indian Ocean
 Territory
Brunei
Bulgaria
Burkina Faso

Burma
Burundi
Cambodia
Cameroon
Canada
Cape Verde
Cayman Islands
Central African Republic
Chad
Chile
China, People's Republic
 of Colombia
Comoros
Congo
Costa Rica
Cote D'Ivoire
Croatia
Cuba
Cyprus
Czech Republic
Denmark
Djibouti
Dominica

Dominican Republic	Greenland
East Timor	Grenada
Eastern Europe	Guadeloupe
Ecuador	Guam
Egypt	Guatemala
El Salvador	Guinea
Equatorial Guinea	Guinea-Bissau
Eritrea	Guyana
Estonia	Haiti
Ethiopia	Honduras
Faeroe Islands	Hong Kong
Falkland Islands	Hungary
Fiji	Iceland
Finland	India
France	Indonesia
Gabon	Iran
The Gambia	Iraq
Georgia	Ireland
Germany	Isle of Man
Ghana	Israel
Gibraltar	Italy
Great Britain	Jamaica
Greece	Japan

Jersey	Malaysia
Jordan	Maldives
Kazakstan	Mali
Kenya	Malta
Kiribati	Marshall Islands
North Korea	Mauritania
South Korea	Mauritius
Kosovo	Mexico
Kuwait	Micronesia
Kyrgyzstan	Moldova
Laos	Monaco
Latvia	Mongolia
Lebanon	Montserrat
Lesotho	Morocco
Liberia	Mozambique
Libya	Myanmar
Liechtenstein	Nagorno-Karabakh
Lithuania	Namibia
Luxembourg	Nauru
Macau	Nepal
Macedonia	Netherlands
Madagascar	New Caledonia
Malawi	New Zealand

Nicaragua
Niger
Nigeria
Niue
Northern Ireland
Northern Mariana Islands
Norway
Oman
Pakistan
Palau
Palestinian Aut.
Panama
Papua New Guinea
Paraguay
Peru
Philippines
Pitcairn Island
Poland
Portugal
Puerto Rico
Qatar
Romania
Russia

Rwanda
St. Helena
St. Kitts & Nevis
St. Lucia
St. Vincent & The
Grenadines
San Marino
São Tomé E Príncipe
Saudi Arabia
Senegal
Serbia
Seychelles
Sierra Leone
Singapore
Slovakia
Slovenia
Soloman Islands
Somalia
South Africa
South Georgia & The
   South Sandwich Islands
Spain
Sri Lanka

Sudan
Suriname
Swaziland
Sweden
Switzerland
Syria
Taiwan
Tajikistan
Tanzania
Thailand
Tibet
Togo
Tonga
Trinidad & Tobago
Tunisia
Turkey
Turkmenistan
Turks & Caicos Islands
Tuvalu
Uganda
Ukraine
United Arab Emirates
United Kingdom

United States of America
Uruguay
Uzbekistan
Vanuatu
Vatican City State
Venezuela
Vietnam
British Virgin Islands
Western Sahara
Western Samoa
Yemen
Yugoslavia
Zaire
Zambia
Zimbabwe

The People of Our Land

Father, in the name of Jesus, we come before You to claim Your promise in 2 Chronicles 7:14 AMP: **If My people, who are called by My name shall humble themselves, pray, seek, crave, and require of necessity My face and turn from their wicked ways, then will I hear from heaven, forgive their sin, and heal their land.**

We are Your people, called by Your name. Thank You for hearing our prayers and moving by Your Spirit in our land. There are famines, earthquakes, floods, natural disasters, and violence occurring. Men's hearts are failing them because of fear.

Lord, Your Son Jesus spoke of discerning the signs of the times. With the Holy Spirit as our Helper, we are watching and praying.

We desire to humble ourselves before You, asking that a spirit of humility be released in us. Thank You for a quiet and meek spirit, for we know that the meek shall inherit the earth.

Search us, O God, and know our hearts; try us, and know our thoughts today. See if there be any wicked way in us, and lead us in the way everlasting.

Forgive us our sins of judging inappropriately, complaining about and criticizing our leaders. Cleanse us with hyssop, and we will be clean; wash us, and we will be whiter than snow. Touch our lips with coals from Your altar that we may pray prayers that avail much for all men and women everywhere.

Lord, we desire to release rivers of living water for the healing of the nations.

In the name of Jesus, amen.

Scripture References

Luke 21:11,25,26	Psalm 51:7 NIV
Matthew 16:3	Isaiah 6:6,7 NIV
Matthew 26:41	James 5:16
James 4:10	1 Timothy 2:1
1 Peter 3:4	John 7:38
Matthew 5:5	Revelation 22:1,2
Psalm 139:23	

American Government

Father, in Jesus' name, we give thanks for the United States and its government. We hold up in prayer before You the men and women who are in positions of authority. We pray and intercede for the president, the representatives, the senators, the judges of our land, the policemen and the policewomen, as well as the governors and mayors, and for all those who are in authority over us in any way. We pray that the Spirit of the Lord rests upon them.

We believe that skillful and godly wisdom has entered into the heart of our president and knowledge is pleasant to him. Discretion watches over him; understanding keeps him and delivers him from the way of evil and from evil men.

Father, we ask that You compass the president about with men and women who make their hearts and ears attentive to godly counsel and do that which is right in Your sight. We believe You cause them to be men and women of integrity who are obedient concerning us that we may lead a quiet and peaceable life in all godliness and honesty. We pray that the upright shall dwell in our government...that men and women blameless and complete in Your sight, Father, shall remain in these positions of authority; but the wicked shall be cut off from our government and the treacherous shall be rooted out of it.

Your Word declares that **blessed is the nation whose God is the Lord** (Ps. 33:12). We receive Your blessing. Father, You are our refuge and stronghold in times of trouble (high cost, destitution, and desperation). So we declare with our mouths that Your people dwell safely in this land, and we *prosper* abundantly. We are more than conquerors through Christ Jesus!

It is written in Your Word that the heart of the king is in the hand of the Lord, and you turn it whichever way You desire. We believe the heart of our leader is in Your hand and that his decisions are divinely directed of the Lord.

We give thanks unto You that the good news of the Gospel is published in our land. The Word of the Lord prevails and grows mightily in the hearts and lives of the people. We give thanks for this land and the leaders You have given to us, in Jesus' name.

Jesus is Lord over the United States! Amen.

Scripture References

1 Timothy 2:1-3   Deuteronomy 28:10,11

Proverbs 2:10-12,21,22 Romans 8:37 AMP

Psalm 33:12   Proverbs 21:1

Psalm 9:9   Acts 12:24

School Systems and Children

Father, we thank You that the entrance of Your Word brings light and thank You that You watch over Your Word to perform it. Father, we bring before You the _____ school system(s) and the men and women who are in positions of authority within the school system(s).

We believe that skillful and godly wisdom has entered into their hearts; that Your knowledge is pleasant to them. Discretion watches over them; understanding keeps them and delivers them from the way of evil and from evil men. We pray that men and women of integrity, blameless, and complete in Your sight, remain in these positions, but that the wicked be cut off and the treacherous be rooted out in the name of Jesus. Father, we thank You for born-again, Spirit-filled people in these positions.

Father, we bring our children, our young people before You. We speak forth Your Word boldly and confidently, Father, that we and our households are saved in the name of Jesus. We are redeemed from the curse of the law for Jesus was made a curse for us. *Our sons and daughters are not given to another people.* We enjoy our children, and they shall not go into captivity, in the name of Jesus.

As parents, we train our children in the way they should go, and when they are old they shall not depart from it.

Our children shrink from whatever might offend You, Father, and discredit the name of Christ. They show themselves to be blameless, guileless, innocent, and uncontaminated children of God without blemish (faultless, unrebukable) in the midst of a crooked and wicked generation, holding out to it and offering to all the Word of Life. Thank You, Father, that You give them knowledge and skill in all learning and wisdom, and bring them into favor with those around them.

Father, we pray and intercede that these young people, their parents, and the leaders in the school system(s) separate themselves from contact with conta-minating and corrupting influences. They cleanse themselves from everything that would contaminate and defile their spirits, souls, and bodies. We confess that they shun immorality and all sexual looseness — flee from impurity in thought, word or deed. They live and conduct themselves honorably and becomingly as in the open light of day. We confess and believe that they shun youthful lusts and flee from them in the name of Jesus.

Satan, we speak to you in the name of Jesus. We bind you, the principalities, the powers, the rulers of the darkness, and wicked spirits in heavenly places and tear down strongholds using the mighty weapons God has provided for us in the name of Jesus. We bind up that blinding spirit of antichrist. We bind every spirit of the occult — astrology, witchcraft, every familiar spirit. We bind sexual immorality, idolatry, obscenity, and profanity. We bind those spirits of alcohol, nicotine, and drug addiction. We bind worldly wisdom in any form — every opposer to the truth. We bind every destructive, deceitful, thieving spirit. You are loosed from your assignment against _____ in the name of Jesus for they escape from the snare of the devil who has held them captive.

We commission the ministering spirits to go forth and police the area dispelling the forces of darkness.

Father, we thank You that in Christ all the treasures of divine wisdom (of comprehensive insight into the ways and purposes of God) and all the riches of spiritual knowledge and enlightenment are stored up and lie hidden for us, and we walk in Him.

We praise You, Father, that we shall see _____ walking in the ways of piety and virtue, revering Your name, Father. Those who err in spirit will come to understanding and those who murmur discontentedly will accept instruction in the Way, Jesus, to Your will and carry out Your purposes in their lives, for You, Father, occupy first place in their hearts. We surround _____ with our faith.

Thank you, Father, that You are the delivering God. Thank You, that the good news of the Gospel is published throughout our school system(s). Thank You for intercessors to stand on Your Word and for laborers of the harvest to preach Your Word in Jesus' name. Praise the Lord! Amen.

Scripture References

Psalm 119:130

Jeremiah 1:12

Proverbs 2:10-12 AMP

Proverbs 2:21,22 AMP

Acts 16:31

Galatians 3:13

Deuteronomy 28:32,41

Proverbs 22:6 AMP

Philippians 2:15,16 AMP

Daniel 1:17 AMP

Daniel 1:9

1 John 2:17 AMP

2 Timothy 2:21 AMP

2 Corinthians 7:1 AMP

1 Corinthians 6:18 AMP

Romans 13:13 AMP

Ephesians 5:4

2 Timothy 2:22

Matthew 18:18

2 Timothy 2:26

Hebrews 1:14

Colossians 2:3 AMP

Isaiah 29:23,24 AMP

Members of the Armed Forces

Father, our troops have been sent into _____ as peacekeepers. We petition You, Lord, according to Psalm 91, for the safety of our military personnel.

This is no afternoon athletic contest that our armed forces will walk away from and forget about in a couple of hours. This is for keeps, a life-or-death fight to the finish against the devil and all his angels. We look beyond human instruments of conflict and address the forces and authorities and rulers of darkness and powers in the spiritual world. As children of the Most High God we enforce the triumphant victory of our Lord Jesus Christ.

Jesus stripped you, Satan, of your principalities and powers, making a show of you openly. Our Lord and Master defeated you. All power and authority both in heaven and earth belong to Him. Righteousness and truth shall prevail. Nations shall come to the light of the Gospel.

We petition heaven to turn our troops into a real peacekeeping force by pouring out the glory of God through our men and women in that part of the world. Use them as instruments of righteousness to defeat the plans of the devil.

Lord, we plead the power of the blood of Jesus, asking You to manifest Your power and glory. We entreat You on behalf of the citizens in these countries on both sides of this conflict. They have experienced pain and heartache; they are victims of the devil's strategies to steal, kill, and destroy. We pray that they will come to know Jesus Who came to give us life, and life more abundantly.

We stand in the gap for the people of the war-torn, devil-overrun land. We expect an overflowing of Your goodness and glory in the lives of those for whom we are praying. May they call upon Your name and be saved.

You, Lord, make known Your salvation; Your righteousness You openly show in the sight of the nations.

Father, provide for and protect the families of our armed forces. Preserve marriages, cause the hearts of the parents to turn toward their children, and the hearts of the children to turn toward the fathers and mothers. We

plead the blood of Jesus over our troops and their families. Provide a support system to undergird, uplift, and
edify those who have been left to raise children by themselves. Jesus has been made unto these parents wisdom,
righteousness, and sanctification. Through Your Holy
Spirit, comfort the lonely and strengthen the weary.

Father, we are looking forward to that day when
the whole earth shall be filled with the knowledge of the
Lord as the waters cover the sea.

In Jesus' name, amen.

Scripture References

Ephesians 6:12 MESSAGE   Psalm 98:2 AMP
Colossians 2:15   Malachi 4:6
John 10:10   1 Corinthians 1:30
Ezekiel 22:30   Isaiah 11:9
Acts 2:21

A portion of this prayer was taken from a letter dated January
22, 1996, written by Kenneth Copeland of Kenneth Copeland
Ministries in Fort Worth, Texas, and sent to his partners. Used
by permission.

The Nation and People of Israel

Lord, You will not cast off nor spurn Your people, neither will You abandon Your heritage. You have regard for the covenant [You made with Abraham]. Father, remember Your covenant with Abraham, Isaac, and Jacob.

Father, we pray for the peace of Jerusalem. May they prosper who love you [the Holy City]. May peace be within your walls and prosperity within your palaces! For our brethren and companions' sake, we will now say, Peace be within you! For the sake of the house of the Lord our God, we will seek, inquire for, and require your good.

Father, we thank You for bringing the people of Israel into unity with each other, and for bringing Your Church (both Jew and Gentile) into oneness — one new man. Thank You for the peace treaties with Israel's former enemies. May these treaties be used for good to make way for the good news of the Gospel as we prepare for the coming of our Messiah.

We intercede for those who have become callously indifferent (blinded, hardened, and made insensible to the Gospel). We pray that they will not fall to their utter spiritual ruin. It was through their false step and transgression that salvation has come to the Gentiles. Now, we ask that the eyes of their understanding be enlightened that they may know the Messiah Who will make Himself known to all of Israel.

We ask You to strengthen the house of Judah and save the house of Joseph. Thank You, Father, for restoring them because You have compassion on them. They will be as though You had not rejected them, for You are the Lord their God, and You will answer them. We thank You for Your great mercy and love to them and to us, in the name of Yeshua, our Messiah.

Father, thank You for saving Israel, and gathering them from the nations, that they may give thanks to Your holy name and glory in Your praise. Praise be to You, Lord, the God of Israel, from everlasting to everlasting. Let all the people say, "Amen!" Praise the Lord.

In Jesus' name, amen.

Scripture References

Psalm 94:14 AMP	Romans 11:7 AMP
Psalm 74:20 AMP	Romans 11:11 AMP
Leviticus 46:22	Ephesians 1:18
Psalm 122:6-9 AMP	Zechariah 10:6,12 NIV
Ephesians 2:14 AMP	Psalm 106:47,48 NIV

Peace of Jerusalem

Father, in the name of Jesus and according to your Word, I long and pray for the peace of Jerusalem, that its inhabitants may be born again. I pray that You, Lord, will be a refuge and a stronghold to the children of Israel. Father, Your Word says "multitudes, multitudes are in the valley of decision" and whoever calls upon Your name shall be delivered and saved. Have mercy upon Israel and be gracious to them, O Lord, and consider that they fight for their land to be restored. You, Lord, are their strength and stronghold in their day of trouble. We pray that they are righteous before You and that You will make even their enemies to be at peace with them. Your Word says You will deliver those for whom we intercede, who are not innocent, through the cleanness of our hands. May they realize that their defense and shield depend on You.

We thank You for Your Word, Lord, that You have a covenant with Israel and that You will take away their sin. They are Your beloved. Your Word also says that

Your gifts are irrevocable, that You never withdraw them once they are given, and that You do not change your mind about those to whom You give Your grace or to whom You send Your call. Though they have been disobedient and rebellious toward You, Lord, we pray that now they will repent and obtain Your mercy and forgiveness through Your Son, Jesus. We praise You, Lord, for Your compassion and Your forgiveness to Your people. We praise You that they are under Your protection and divine guidance, that they are Your special possession, Your peculiar treasure, and that You will spare them, for we have read in Your Word that all Israel shall be saved!

Thank You, Father, for delivering us all from every evil work and the authority You have given us with the name of Jesus. We love You and praise You. Every day, with its new reasons, do we praise You!

Pray for the peace of Jerusalem! May they prosper that love you "the Holy City"! Peace be within your walls and prosperity within your palaces! Amen.

Scripture References

Joel 3:14	Romans 11:29
Job 22:30 AMP	Isaiah 45:17

Spirit-Controlled Life

The law of the Spirit of life in Christ Jesus has made _____ free from the law of sin and death. His/her life is governed, not by the standards and according to the dictates of the flesh, but controlled by the Holy Spirit. _____ is not living the life of the flesh. _____ is living the life of the Spirit. The Holy Spirit of God dwells within, and directs and controls him/her.

_____ is a conqueror and gains a surpassing victory through Jesus Who loved him/her. _____ does not let himself/herself be overcome by evil, but overcomes and masters evil with good. _____ has on the full armor of light. _____ clothes himself/herself with the Lord Jesus Christ, the Messiah, and makes no provision for indulging the flesh.

_____ is a doer of God's Word. He/she has God's wisdom. He/she is peace-loving, courteous, considerate, gentle, willing to yield to reason, full of compassion and good fruits. _____ is free from doubts, wavering, and insincerity. He/she is subject to God.

_____ stands firm against the devil.
_____ resists the devil and he flees from him/her.
_____ comes close to God and God comes close to him/her. _____ does not fear for God never leaves him.

In Christ, _____ is filled with the Godhead: Father, Son, and Holy Spirit. Jesus is his/her Lord!

In the name of Jesus, amen.

Scripture References

Romans 8:2,4,9,14,31,37 AMP   James 3:17 AMP

Romans 12:21   Hebrews 13:5

Romans 13:12,14   James 4:7,8

James 1:22   Colossians 2:10

Renew Fellowship

Father, You hasten Your Word to perform it. I believe and confess that _____ is a disciple of Christ, taught of You, Lord, and obedient to Your will. Great is his/her peace and undisturbed composure. _____ has You in person for his/her teacher. He/she has listened and learned from You and has come to Jesus.

_____ continues to hold to things he/she has learned and of which he/she is convinced. From childhood he/she has had knowledge of and been acquainted with the Word, which is able to instruct him/her and give him/her the understanding of the salvation which comes through faith in Christ Jesus. Father, You will heal _____, lead _____, and recompense _____, and restore comfort to _____.

Jesus gives _____ eternal life. He/she shall never lose it or perish throughout the ages, to all eternity. _____ shall never by any means be destroyed. You, Father, have given _____ to Jesus. You are

PRAYERS THAT AVAIL MUCH COMMEMORATIVE GIFT EDITION

greater and mightier than all else; no one is able to snatch _____ out of Your hand.

I pray and believe that _____ comes to his/her senses and escapes out of the snare of the devil who has held him/her captive; and that _____ would judge himself/herself.

In the name of Jesus, Satan and every hindering spirit, you are bound in _____'s life.

_____ has become a fellow-heir with Christ, the Messiah, and shares in all He has for him/her and holds the first newborn confidence and original assured expectation firm and unshaken to the end. _____ casts not away his/her confidence for it has great recompense of reward.

Thank You for giving _____ wisdom and revelation — quickening him/her to Your Word. Thank You that _____ enjoys fellowship with You and Jesus and with fellow believers.

In Jesus' name, amen.

Scripture References

Jeremiah 1:12	2 Timothy 2:26 AMP
John 6:45	1 Corinthians 11:31
Isaiah 54:13 AMP	Matthew 18:18
2 Timothy 3:14,15	Hebrews 3:14 AMP
Isaiah 57:18	Hebrews 10:35 AMP
John 10:28,29	Ephesians 1:17
1 John 5:16	1 John 1:3

Deliverance From Satan and His Demonic Forces

If the person for whom you are interceding has not confessed Jesus as Savior and Lord, pray specifically for his/her salvation if you have not already done so. Stand and thank the Father that it is done in the name of Jesus. Then pray:

Father, in the name of Jesus, I come boldly to Your throne of grace and present _____ before You. I stand in the gap and intercede in behalf of _____ knowing that the Holy Spirit within me takes hold together with me against the evils that would attempt to hold _____ in bondage. I unwrap _____ from the bonds of wickedness with my prayers and take my shield of faith and quench every fiery dart of the adversary that would come against _____.

Father, You say that whatever I bind on earth is bound in heaven, and whatever I loose on earth is loosed in heaven. You say for me to cast out demons in the name of Jesus.

So I speak to you, Satan, and to the principalities, the powers, the rulers of the darkness, and spiritual wickedness in

high places and the demonic spirits of_____
(names of spirits) assigned to _____. I take authority over
you and bind you away from _____ in the mighty
name of Jesus. You loose _____ and let him/her go free
in the name of Jesus. I demand that you desist in your
maneuvers now. Satan, you are a spoiled and defeated foe.

Ministering spirits of God, you go forth in the name of Jesus and provide the necessary help to and assistance for _____.

Father, I have laid hold of _____'s salvation and his/her confession of the Lordship of Jesus Christ. I speak of things that are not as though they were, for I choose to look at the unseen — the eternal things of God. I say that Satan shall not get an advantage over _____: for I am not ignorant of Satan's devices. I resist Satan and he has run in terror from _____ in the name of Jesus. I give Satan no place in _____. I plead the blood of the Lamb over _____ for Satan and his cohorts are overcome by that blood and Your Word. I thank You, Father, that I tread on serpents and scorpions and over all the power of the enemy in _____'s behalf. _____ is delivered from this present evil world. He/she is delivered from the powers of darkness and translated into the Kingdom of Your dear Son!

Father, I ask You now to fill those vacant places within _____ with Your redemption, Your Word, Your Holy Spirit, Your love, Your wisdom, Your righteousness, and Your revelation knowledge in the name of Jesus.

I thank You, Father, that _____ is redeemed by the blood of Jesus out of the hand of Satan. He/she is justified and made righteous by the blood of Jesus and belongs to You — spirit, soul, and body. I thank You that every enslaving yoke is broken, for he/she will not become the slave of anything or be brought under its power in the name of Jesus. _____ has escaped the snare of the devil who has held him/her captive and henceforth does Your will, Father, which is to glorify You in his/her spirit, soul, and body.

Thank You, Father, that Jesus was manifested that He might destroy the works of the devil. Satan's works are destroyed in _____'s life in the name of Jesus. Hallelujah! _____ walks in the Kingdom of God

which is righteousness, peace, and joy in the Holy
Spirit! Praise the Lord! Amen.

*Once this prayer has been prayed, thank the Father that
Satan and his cohorts are bound. Stand firm, fixed, immovable, and steadfast on your confessions of faith as you intercede on this person's behalf for* **greater is he that is in you,
than he that is in the world** (1 John 4:4).

Scripture References

Hebrews 4:16	2 Corinthians 2:11
Ezekiel 22:30	James 4:7
Romans 8:26	Ephesians 4:27
Isaiah 58:6	Revelation 12:11
Ephesians 6:16	Luke 10:19
Matthew 18:18	Galatians 1:4
Mark 16:17	Colossians 1:13
Ephesians 6:12	Matthew 12:43-45
Colossians 2:15	1 Corinthians 6:12
Matthew 12:29	2 Timothy 2:26
Hebrews 1:14	1 John 3:8
Romans 4:17	Romans 14:17
2 Corinthians 4:18	

Deliverance From Cults

Father, in the name of Jesus, we come before You in prayer and in faith believing that Your Word runs swiftly throughout the earth, for the Word of God is not chained or imprisoned. We bring before You

_____(those, and families of those, involved in cults).

Father, stretch forth Your hand from above, rescue and deliver _____ out of great waters, from the land of hostile aliens whose mouths speak deceit and whose right hands are right hands raised in taking fraudulent oaths. Their mouths must be stopped for they are mentally distressing and subverting _____ and whole families by teaching what they ought not teach, for the purpose of getting base advantage and disreputable gain. But praise God, they will not get very far for their rash folly will become obvious to everybody!

Execute justice, precious Father, for the oppressed. Set the prisoners free, open the eyes of the blind, lift up the bowed down, heal the brokenhearted, and bind up their wounds. Lift up the humble and downtrodden and cast the wicked down to the ground in the mighty name of Jesus.

Turn back the hearts of the disobedient, incredulous, and unpersuadable to the wisdom of the upright, and the knowledge of the will of God, in order to make ready for You, Lord, a people perfectly prepared in spirit, adjusted, disposed, and placed in the right moral state.

Father, You say in Your Word to refrain our voices from weeping and our eyes from tears, for our prayers shall be rewarded and _____ shall return from the enemy's land and come again to his/her own country. You will save our offspring from the land of their exile; from the east and the west — sons from afar and daughters from the ends of the earth. We shall see _____ walking in the ways of piety and virtue, revering Your name, Father. Those who err in spirit will come to understanding. Those who murmur discontentedly will accept instruction in the Way, Jesus. Father, You contend with those who contend with us, and You give safety to _____.

Satan, we speak to you in the name of Jesus. We bind you, the principalities, the powers, the rulers of the darkness, and the wicked spirits in heavenly places, and we tear down strongholds using the mighty weapons God has provided for us in the name of Jesus. We speak to greed, selfishness, pride, arrogance, boastfulness, abuse, blasphemy, disobedience, ungratefulness, profanity, rebellion, perverseness, slander, immorality, ferocity, hatred, treachery, conceit, lust, material-ism, error, deceit, spirit of antichrist, unworthiness, filthiness, cruelty, hostility, depravity, distortion, ungodliness, and falsity and loose you from all diabolical assignments against _____. We cancel all negative talking and doubt and unbelief. Satan, you will not use this against _____.

We commission the ministering spirits to go forth and dispel these forces of darkness and bring _____ home in the name of Jesus.

Father, we believe and confess that _____ has had knowledge of and been acquainted with the Word which was able to instruct him/her and give him/her the understanding for salvation which comes through faith in Christ Jesus. Lord, we pray and believe that You

certainly will deliver _____ and draw _____
to Yourself from every assault of evil and preserve and
bring _____ safe into Your heavenly Kingdom.
Glory to You, Father, Who delivers those for whom we
intercede in Jesus' name! Amen.

Once this prayer has been prayed for an individual,
confess it as done. Thank the Father that he or she is deliv-
ered, returning from the enemy's land. Thank God that
Satan is bound. Thank God for his/her salvation.

Scripture References

Psalm 147:15	Isaiah 43:5,6
2 Timothy 2:9	Isaiah 29:23,24
Psalm 144:7,8	Isaiah 49:25
Titus 1:11	Matthew 18:18
2 Timothy 3:9	2 Timothy 3:2-9
Psalm 146:7,8	Hebrews 1:14
Psalm 147:3-6	2 Timothy 3:15
Luke 1:17	2 Timothy 4:18
Jeremiah 31:16,17	Job 22:30
Jeremiah 46:27	

Deliverance From Habits

Father, in the name of Jesus and according to Your Word, I hereby believe in my heart and say with my mouth that Jesus is the Lord of _____'s life. I also confess that from this day forward _____ is set free and delivered from the habit(s) of _____ in the name of Jesus.

Satan, you and all your principalities, powers, and master spirits who rule the darkness, and spiritual wickedness in high places are bound up and _____ is loosed from you in the name of Jesus, as it is written in Matthew 18:18-19. No longer can you, Satan, harass or operate any of your unclean spirits or habits over _____. He/she will not become the slave of anything that exalts itself over the Word of God or be brought under its power.

I hereby confess that _____ is strengthened and reinforced with mighty power in his/her innerself by the Holy Spirit Who lives and dwells in his/her innermost being. _____ is strong in the Lord.

Deliverance From Corrupt Companions

Satan, in Jesus' name, take your hands off _____.
I bind you from his/her life. You desist in your maneuvers
against him/her.

Father, I thank You for delivering _____
from corrupt and depraved people. I confess that
_____ has awakened and returned to sober sense
and his/her right mind, and sins no more. _____
separates himself/herself from contact with contaminat-
ing influences and cleanses himself/herself from everything that would defile his/her spirit, soul, and body.

_____ lives and conducts himself/herself
honorably and becomingly as in the open light of day;
not in reveling (carousing) and drunkenness, not in
immorality and debauchery (sensuality and licentious-
ness), not in quarreling and jealousy. _____ is
done with every trace of wickedness (depravity, malig-
nity) and all deceit and insincerity (pretense, hypocrisy,
grudges, slander), and evil speaking of every kind.

_____ is loyally subject (submissive) to the governing (civil) authorities — not resisting nor setting himself/herself up against them. _____ is obedient, prepared, and willing to do any upright and honorable work. _____ walks as a companion with wise men, and he/she shall be wise.

His/her sins have been forgiven. _____ is pardoned through the name of Jesus and because of confessing His name. _____ is victorious over the wicked one because he/she has come to know and recognize and be aware of the Father.

The Word dwells and remains in _____ and he/she dwells in the Son and in the Father always. God's nature abides in _____ — His principle of life remains permanently within _____ and he/she cannot practice sinning because he/she is born of God The law of the Spirit of life in Christ Jesus has made _____ free from the law of sin and death. Thank You, Father, for watching over Your Word to perform it in Jesus' name! Amen.

Scripture References

1 Corinthians 15:33,34a
2 Timothy 2:21
2 Corinthians 7:1
Romans 13:13
1 Peter 2:1
Romans 13:1,2
Titus 3:1
Proverbs 13:20

Proverbs 28:7
1 Thessalonians 5:22
1 John 2:12-16
1 John 2:21,24
1 John 3:9
Romans 8:2
Jeremiah 1:12

Deliverance From Mental Disorder

Father, in the name of Jesus, I fearlessly and confidently and boldly draw near to the throne of grace; that I may receive mercy and find grace to help in good time for _____.

It is my prayer that _____ will come to the knowledge of the truth and be saved from destruction. Father, according to Psalm 107:20, You sent Your Word and healed _____ and delivered him/her from all his/her destructions. I am calling upon You in the day of trouble, asking You to deliver _____, and in the name of Jesus he/she shall honor and glorify You. Father, I thank You for delivering his/her soul from death, and his/her feet from falling, so that he/she may walk before You in the light of the living.

It is You, Father, Who delivers _____ from the pit and corruption of _____ *(name of disorder: schizophrenia, paranoia, manic depression, etc.).* Father, You have not given _____ a spirit of timidity — of

DELIVERANCE FROM MENTAL DISORDER

cowardice, of craven and cringing and fawning fear —
but [You have given him/her a spirit of] power and of
love and of calm and well-balanced mind and discipline
and self-control.

In the name of Jesus, I forgive his/her sins and
stand in the gap for him/her until he/she comes to
his/her senses [and] escapes out of the snare of the devil,
who has held him/her captive.

*Satan, I stand against you, your principalities, and
powers, your rulers of the darkness of this world, and spiritual
wickedness in high places which have been assigned to
_____. It is our God Who delivers from the authority
of darkness, and translates into the Kingdom of His dear Son.*

I decree and declare that the law of the Spirit of life
in Christ Jesus has made _____ free from the law
of sin and death. _____ shall no longer be of two
minds — hesitating, dubious, irresolute — unstable and
unreliable and uncertain about everything (he/she
thinks, feels, and decides). _____ shall get rid of
all uncleanness and the rampant outgrowth of wickedness, and in a humble (gentle, modest) spirit receive and

welcome the Word which implanted and rooted [in his/her heart] contains the power to save his/her soul (mind, will, and emotions).

In the name of Jesus, grace be to _____ and peace from God our Father, and from the Lord Jesus Christ, Who gave Himself for his/her sin so that He might deliver him/her from this present evil world, according to the will of God, and our Father, to Whom be glory for ever and ever. Amen.

Scripture References

Hebrews 4:16 AMP	2 Timothy 2:26 AMP
Psalm 50:15	Ephesians 6:12
Psalm 56:13	Colossians 1:13
Psalm 103:4a AMP	Romans 8:2
2 Timothy 1:7 AMP	James 1:8,21 AMP
John 20:23 AMP	Galatians 1:3-5

Hedge of Protection

Father, in the name of Jesus, we lift up _____
to You and pray a hedge of protection around him/her.
We thank You, Father, that You are a wall of fire round
about _____ and that you set Your angels round
about him/her.

We thank You, Father, that _____ dwells in
the secret place of the Most High and abides under the
shadow of the Almighty. We say of You, Lord, You are
his/her refuge and fortress, in You will he/she trust. You
cover _____ with Your feathers, and under Your
wings shall he/she trust. _____ shall not be afraid
of the terror by night or the arrow that flies by day. Only
with his/her eyes will _____ behold and see the
reward of the wicked.

Because _____ has made You, Lord, his/her
refuge and fortress, no evil shall befall him/her — no
accident will overtake him/her — neither shall any
plague or calamity come near him/her. For You give

Your angels charge over _____, to keep him/her in all Your ways.

Father, because You have set Your love upon _____, therefore will You deliver him/her. _____ shall call upon You, and You will answer him/her. You will be with him/her in trouble, and will satisfy _____ with a long life and show him/her Your salvation. Not a hair of his/her head shall perish. Amen.

Scripture References

Zechariah 2:5   Psalm 91:8-11 AMP

Psalm 34:7   Psalm 91:14-16 AMP

Psalm 91:1,2 AMP   Luke 21:18

Psalm 91:4,5 AMP

_____ lets this same attitude and purpose and humble mind be in him/her which was in Christ Jesus. Thank You, Father, in Jesus' name. Amen.

Scripture References (AMP)

Isaiah 54:13   Psalm 119:36

Ephesians 4:23,24   1 John 2:15,16,21

Ephesians 4:15   Proverbs 4:8,20-23

Proverbs 8:6-8   Philippians 2:2

Employment

Father, in Jesus' name, we believe and confess Your Word over _____ today knowing that You watch over Your Word to perform it. Your Word prospers in _____ whereto it is sent! Father, You are his/her source of every consolation, comfort, and encouragement. _____ is courageous and grows in strength.

His/her desire is to owe no man anything but to love him. Therefore, _____ is strong and lets not his/her hands be weak or slack, for his/her work shall be rewarded. His/her wages are not counted as a favor or a gift, but as something owed to him. _____ makes it his/her ambition and definitely endeavors to live quietly and peacefully, minds his/her own affairs, and works with his/her hands. He/she is correct and honorable and commands the respect of the outside world, being self-supporting, dependent on nobody and having need of nothing, for You, Father, supply to the full his/her every need.

He/she works in quietness, earns his/her own food and other necessities. He/she is not weary of doing right and continues in well-doing without weakening.

_____ learns to apply himself/herself to good deeds — to honest labor and honorable employment — so that he/she is able to meet necessary demands whenever the occasion may require.

Father, You know the record of his/her works and what he/she is doing. You have set before _____ a door wide open, which no one is able to shut.

_____ does not fear and is not dismayed, for You, Father, strengthen him/her. You, Father, help _____ in Jesus' name, for in Jesus _____ has perfect peace and confidence and is of good cheer, for Jesus overcame the world and deprived it of its power to harm _____. He/she does not fret or have anxiety about anything, for Your peace, Father, mounts guard over his/her heart and mind. _____ knows the secret of facing every situation, for he/she is self-sufficient in Christ's sufficiency. _____ guards his/her mouth and his/her tongue keeping himself/herself from trouble.

_____ prizes Your wisdom, Father, and acknowledges You. You direct, make straight and plain his/her path, and You promote him/her. Therefore, Father, _____ increases in Your wisdom (in broad and full understanding), and in stature and years, and in favor with You, Father and with man! Amen.

Scripture References

Jeremiah 1:12

Isaiah 55:11

2 Corinthians 1:3 AMP

1 Corinthians 16:13

Romans 13:8 AMP

2 Chronicles 15:7 AMP

Romans 4:4 AMP

1 Thessalonians 4:11,12 AMP

2 Thessalonians 3:12,13 AMP

Titus 3:14 AMP

Revelation 3:8 AMP

Isaiah 41:10 AMP

John 16:33 AMP

Philippians 4:6,7 AMP

Philippians 4:12,13 AMP

Proverbs 21:23 AMP

Proverbs 3:6 AMP

Proverbs 4:8 AMP

Luke 2:52 AMP

Overcoming Negative Work Attitudes

Thank You, Father, in Jesus' name, for watching over Your Word to perform it. _____ is obedient to his/her employers — bosses or supervisors — having respect for them and eager to please them, in singleness of motive and with all his/her heart, as service to Christ, not in the way of eye service — as if they were watching him/her — but as a servant (employee) of Christ, doing the will of God heartily and with his/her whole soul.

_____ readily renders service with goodwill, as to the Lord and not to men. He/she knows that for whatever good he/she does, he/she will receive his/her reward from the Lord.

_____ will do all things without grumbling, faultfinding, and complaining against God, and questioning and doubting within himself/herself. He/she is blameless and harmless, a child of God, without rebuke, in the midst of a crooked and perverse nation, among whom he/she shines as a light in the world.

He/she reveres the Lord, and his/her work is a sincere expression of his/her devotion to Him. Whatever may be his/her task, he/she works at it heartily from the soul, as something done for God. The One Whom _____ is actually serving is the Lord. Amen.

Scripture References (AMP)

Ephesians 6:5-8   Philippians 2:14,15
Colossians 3:22-24

Prosperity

Father, in the name of Jesus, I praise You with my whole heart. I praise You for Your mighty acts, and according to the abundance of Your greatness! Through faith in the name of Jesus, I say that _____ has received and enjoys life — and has it in abundance — to the full, till it overflows!

Father, according to Your Word, it is Your desire that _____ may prosper and be in health, even as his/her soul prospers. In the name of Jesus, I declare that _____ gets rid of all uncleanness and the rampant outgrowth of wickedness, and in a humble (gentle, modest) spirit receives and welcomes the Word which implanted and rooted [in his/her heart] contains the power to save his/her soul. In the name of Jesus, I affirm that he/she will diligently obey the message; being a doer of the Word, and not merely a listener to it.

I state that his/her delight and desire are in the law of the Lord, and on His law — the precepts, the instructions, the teachings of God — he/she habitually meditates (ponders and studies) by day and by night.

Then he/she shall be like a tree firmly planted [and tended] by the streams of water, ready to bring forth his/her fruit in his/her season; his/her leaf also shall not fade or wither, and everything he/she does shall prosper [and come to maturity].

Holy Spirit, Jesus said that You will bring all things to his/her remembrance. Therefore, I decree that he/she will (earnestly) remember the Lord his/her God; for it is You Who give _____ power to get wealth, that You may establish Your covenant which You swore to our fathers.

Father, I attest that out of the abundance of his/her heart _____ shall say continually, Let the Lord be magnified, Who takes pleasure in the prosperity of His servant. And his/her tongue shall talk of Your righteousness, rightness, and justice, and [his/her reason for] Your praise all the day long. Amen.

Scripture References

Psalm 9:1   Psalm 1:2,3 AMP

Psalm 150:2 AMP   John 14:26b

John 10:10b AMP   Deuteronomy 8:18 AMP
3 John 2   Matthew 12:34
James 1:21,22 AMP   Psalm 35:27b,28 AMP

Single Believer

_____ is united to the Lord and has become one spirit with Him. _____ shuns immorality and all sexual looseness. _____ flees from impurity in thought, word, or deed.

_____ will not sin against his/her body by committing sexual immorality. His/her body is the temple of the Holy Spirit, Whom he/she has received as a gift from God. _____ is not his/her own. _____ was bought for a price and made God's own. _____ will honor God and bring glory to Him in his/her spirit, soul, and body which are God's.

_____ shuns youthful lusts and flees from them, and aims at and pursues righteousness — all that is virtuous and good, right living, conformity to the will of God in thought, word, and deed. He/she aims at and pursues faith, love, and peace — which is harmony and concord with others — in fellowship with all Christians, who call upon the name of the Lord out of a pure heart.

_____ shrinks from whatever might offend You, Father, or discredit the name of Christ.

_____ shows himself/herself to be a blameless, guileless, innocent, and uncontaminated child of God without blemish (faultless) in the midst of a crooked and wicked generation, among whom _____ is seen as a bright light shining out clearly in the dark world, holding out to it and offering to all the Word of Life. Thank You, Father, that Jesus is Lord.

In Jesus' name, amen.

Scripture References

1 Corinthians 6:17-20   Philippians 2:12,15,16
2 Timothy 2:22

Complete in Him as a Single

Father, we thank You that _____ desires and earnestly seeks first after the things of Your Kingdom. We thank You that he/she knows that You love him/her and that he/she can trust Your Word.

For in Jesus the whole fullness of Deity (the Godhead) continues to dwell in bodily form — giving complete expression of the Divine Nature, and _____ is in Him and has come to the fullness of life in Christ. He/she is filled with the Godhead — Father, Son, and Holy Spirit — and he/she reaches full spiritual stature. And Christ is the head of all rule and authority — of every angelic principality and power.

So because of Jesus, _____ is complete; Jesus is his/her Lord. He/she comes before You, Father, desiring a born-again Christian mate. We petition that Your will be done in his/her life. Now we enter into that blessed rest by adhering, trusting in, and relying on You, in the name of Jesus. Amen.

Scripture References (AMP)

Colossians 2:9,10   Hebrews 4:10

Single Female Trusting God for a Mate

Father, in the name of Jesus, I believe that You are providing Your very best for _____. And the man who will be united with _____ in marriage has awakened to righteousness. Father, as You have rejoiced over Jerusalem, so shall the bridegroom rejoice over _____. Thank You, Father, that he will love _____ as Christ loves the Church. He will nourish, carefully protect, and cherish _____.

Father, I believe, because he is Your best, that doubts, wavering, and insincerity are not a part of him; but he speaks forth the oracles of God, acknowledging Your full counsel with all wisdom and knowledge. He does not speak or act contrary to the Word. He walks totally in love, esteeming and preferring others higher than himself.

Father, I believe that everything not of You shall be removed from _____'s life. And, I thank You for the perfecting of Your Word in her life that she may be thoroughly furnished unto all good works. Father, I praise You for the performance of Your Word in her behalf. Amen.

Scripture References

Isaiah 62:5   James 3:17

Ephesians 5:25   Proverbs 8:8

Single Male Trusting God for a Mate

Father, in the name of Jesus, I believe that You are providing a suitable helpmate for _____. Father, according to Your Word, one who will adapt herself to _____, respect, honor, prefer, and esteem him, stand firmly by his side, united in spirit and purpose, having the same love and being in full accord and of one harmonious mind and intention.

Father, You say in Your Word that a wise, understanding, and prudent wife is from You, and he who finds a true wife finds a good thing and obtains favor of You.

Father, I know that _____ has found favor in Your sight, and I praise You and thank You for Your Word, knowing that You watch over it to perform it. Amen.

Scripture References

Ephesians 5:22,33   Proverbs 19:14
Proverbs 18:22   Philippians 2:2

Peace in a Troubled Marriage

Father, in the name of Jesus, we bring _____ before You. We pray and confess Your Word over them, and as we do, we use our faith, believing that Your Word will come to pass.

Therefore we pray and confess that _____ will let all bitterness, indignation, wrath, passion, rage, bad temper, resentment, brawling, clamor, contention, slander, abuse, evil speaking, or blasphemous language be banished from them; also all malice, spite, ill will, or baseness of any kind. We pray that _____ have become useful and helpful and kind to each other, tenderhearted, compassionate, understanding, loving-hearted, forgiving one another readily and freely as You Father, in Christ, forgave them.

Therefore, _____ will be imitators of You, God. They will copy You and follow Your example as well-beloved children imitate their father. _____ will walk in love, esteeming and delighting in one another as Christ loved them and gave Himself up for them, a slain offering and sacrifice to You God, so that it became a sweet fragrance.

Satan, we render you helpless in your activities in the lives of_____ . We come against the spirit of separation and divorce, and we loose you from your assignment against them. Satan, your power is broken from their marriage in the name of Jesus.

Father, we thank You that _____ will be constantly renewed in the spirit of their minds having a fresh mental and spiritual attitude. They have put on the new nature and are created in God's image in true righteousness and holiness. They have come to their senses and escaped out of the snare of the devil who has held them captive and henceforth will do Your will, which is that they love one another with the God-kind of love, united in total peace and harmony and happiness.

Thank You for the answer, Lord. We know it is done now in the name of Jesus. Amen.

Scripture References

Ephesians 4:31,32 AMP Ephesians 4:23,24

Ephesians 5:1,2   2 Timothy 2:26 AMP

Matthew 18:18

Overcoming Infidelity

Father, I thank You that You hear my prayer, for I come in the name of Jesus and on the authority of Your Word. I come boldly to the throne of grace to receive mercy and find grace to help on behalf of _____ and _____. I take my place — standing in the gap — against the devil and his demons until the salvation of God is manifested in their lives. Father, I forgive them for their sins and stand firm knowing that the Holy Spirit will convict and convince them of sin, righteousness and judgment.

The wife, _____, is sane and sober-minded, temperate, and disciplined. She loves her husband and their children, and she confines herself to them. She is self-controlled, chaste, good-natured and kindhearted, adapting and subordinating herself to her husband, that the Word of God may not be exposed to reproach — blasphemed or discredited.

In a similar way, her husband, _____, is self-restrained and prudent, taking life seriously. He drinks waters out of his own cistern [of pure marriage relationship], and fresh running waters out of his own well — lest his offspring be dispersed abroad as waterbrooks in the street. He confines himself to his own wife, and their children will be for them alone and not the children of strangers with them. His fountain of human life is blessed with the rewards of fidelity, and he rejoices with the wife of his youth. He lets his wife be to him as the loving hind and pleasant doe [tender, gentle, attractive]. He lets her bosom satisfy him at all times; and he is transported with delight in her love.

The husband submits himself to Christ, Who is the head of the man. The husband is the head of his own wife, and they are subject one to the other out of reverence for Christ.

Thank You, Father, for hearing my prayer on behalf of this family. I know that You watch over Your Word to perform it, in Jesus' name. Amen.

Scripture References (AMP)

Titus 2:4-6	1 Corinthians 11:3
Proverbs 5:15-19	Ephesians 5:21
Hebrews 9:14	Jeremiah 1:12

Overcoming Rejection in Marriage

Father, in the name of Jesus, _____ and _____ are delivered from this present evil age by the Son of the Living God, and whom the Son has set free is free indeed. Therefore, they are delivered from a spirit of rejection and accepted in the Beloved to be holy and blameless in His sight. They forgive all those who have wronged them, and their hurts from the past are healed, for Jesus came to heal the brokenhearted.

They are God's chosen people, holy and dearly loved. They clothe themselves with compassion, kindness, humility, gentleness, and patience. They bear with each other and forgive whatever grievances they may have against one another. They forgive as the Lord forgave them. Over all these virtues, they put on love, which binds them together in perfect unity.

When they were children, they talked like children, thought like children, and reasoned like children, but now they have become husband and wife, and they are done with childish ways and have put them aside. The blood of Christ, Who through the eternal Spirit offered Himself without spot to God, purges their consciences from dead works of selfishness, agitating passions, and moral conflicts, so they can serve the Living God. They touch not any unclean thing, for they are a son and daughter of the Most High God. Satan's power over them is broken and his strongholds are torn down. Sin no longer has dominion over them and their household.

The love of God reigns supreme in their home, and the peace of God acts as an umpire in all situations, Jesus is their Lord — spirit, soul, and body. Amen.

Scripture References (AMP)

Galatians 1:4	Romans 6:18
John 8:36	Colossians 3:12-15
Ephesians 1:16	1 Corinthians 13:11
Luke 4:18	1 Thessalonians 5:23

Children at School

Father, in Jesus' name, I confess Your Word this day concerning my children as they pursue their education and training at school. You are effectually at work in them creating within them the power and desire to please You. They are the head and not the tail, above and not beneath.

I pray that my children will find favor, good understanding and high esteem in the sight of God and their teachers and classmates. I ask You to give my children wisdom and understanding as knowledge is presented to them in all fields of study and endeavor.

Father, thank You for giving my children an appreciation for education and helping them to understand that the Source and beginning of all knowledge is You. They have the appetite of the diligent and they are abundantly supplied with educational resources, and their thoughts are those of the steadily diligent which tend only to achievement. Thank You that they are growing in wisdom and knowledge. I will not cease to pray for them, asking that they be filled with the knowledge of Your will bearing fruit in every good work.

Father, I thank You that my children have divine protection since they dwell in the secret place of the Most High. My children trust and find their refuge in You and stand rooted and grounded in Your love. They shall not be led astray by philosophies of men and teaching that is contrary to Truth. You are their shield and buckler protecting them from attacks or threats. Thank You for the angels which You have assigned to them to accompany, defend and preserve them in all their ways of obedience and service. My children are established in Your love which drives all fear out of doors.

I pray that the teachers of my children will be godly men and women of integrity. Give our teachers understanding hearts and wisdom in order that they may walk in the ways of piety and virtue, revering Your holy name. Amen.

Scripture References

Philippians 2:13   Psalm 91:1,2

Deuteronomy 28:1,2,13   Ephesians 4:14
Proverbs 3:4   Psalm 91:3-11
1 Kings 4:29   Ephesians 1:17
Daniel 1:4   Psalm 112:8
Proverbs 1:4,7   Ephesians 3:17
Proverbs 3:13   Matthew 18:18
Proverbs 4:5   James 1:5
Colossians 1:9,10

Child's Future

Father, Your Word declares that children are an inheritance from You and promises peace when they are taught in Your ways. I dedicate _____ to You today, that he/she might be raised as You would desire and will follow the path You would choose. Father, I confess Your Word this day over _____. I thank You that Your Word goes out and will not return unto You void, but will accomplish what it says it will do.

Heavenly Father, I commit myself, as a parent, to train _____ in the way he/she should go, trusting in the promise that he/she will not depart from Your ways, but will grow and prosper in them. I turn the care and burden of raising him/her over to You. I will not provoke my child, but will nurture and love him/her in Your care. I will do as the Word of God commands and teach my child diligently. My child will be upon my heart and mind. Your grace is sufficient to overcome my inabilities as a parent.

My child _____ is obedient and honors both his/her parents, being able to accept the abundant promises of Your Word of long life and prosperity.

_____ is a godly child; not ashamed or afraid to honor and keep Your Word. He/she stands convinced that You are the Almighty God. I am thankful that as _____ grows, he/she will remember You and not pass by the opportunity of a relationship with Your Son, Jesus. Your great blessings will be upon _____ for keeping Your ways. I thank You for Your blessings over every area of _____'s life, that You will see to the salvation and obedience of his/her life to Your ways.

Heavenly Father, I thank You now that laborers will be sent into _____'s path, preparing the way for salvation, as it is written in Your Word, through Your Son, Jesus. I am thankful that _____ will recognize the traps of the devil and will be delivered to salvation through the purity of Your Son. You have given _____ the grace and the strength to walk the narrow pathway to Your Kingdom.

I pray that just as Jesus increased in wisdom and stature, You would bless this child with the same wisdom and pour out Your favor and wisdom openly to him/her.

I praise You in advance for _____'s future spouse. Father, Your Word declares that you desire for children to be pure and honorable, waiting upon marriage. I speak blessings to the future union and believe that _____ will be well suited to his/her partner and their household will be in godly order, holding fast to the love of Jesus Christ. Continue to prepare _____ to be the man/woman of God that You desire him/her to be.

_____ shall be diligent and hard-working, never being lazy or undisciplined. Your Word promises great blessing to his/her house and he/she shall always be satisfied and will always increase. Godliness is profitable unto his/her house, and _____ shall receive the promise of life and all that is to come.

Father, thank You for protecting and guiding my child.

In Jesus' name I pray, amen.

Scripture References

Psalm 127:3	Matthew 7:14
Isaiah 54:13	Luke 2:52
Isaiah 55:11	Hebrews 13:4
Proverbs 22:6	1 Thessalonians 4:3
1 Peter 5:7	Ephesians 5:22-25
Ephesians 6:4	2 Timothy 1:13
Deuteronomy 6:7	Proverbs 13:11
2 Corinthians 12:9	Proverbs 20:13
Ephesians 6:1-3	Romans 12:11
2 Timothy 1:12	1 Timothy 4:8
Proverbs 8:17,32	1 John 3:8
Luke 19:10	John 10:10
Matthew 9:38	Matthew 18:18
2 Corinthians 2:11	John 14:13
2 Timothy 2:26	Psalm 91:1,11
Job 22:30	

Prayer for a Teenager

Father, in the name of Jesus, I affirm Your Word over my son/daughter. I commit _____ to you and delight myself also in You. I thank You that You deliver _____ out of rebellion into right relationship with us, his/her parents.

Father, the first commandment with a promise is to the child who obeys his/her parents in the Lord. You said that all will be well with him/her and he/she will live long on the earth. I affirm this promise on behalf of my child asking You to give _____ an obedient spirit that he/she may honor (esteem and value as precious) his/her father and mother.

Father, forgive me for mistakes made out of my own unresolved hurts or selfishness which may have caused _____ hurt. I release the anointing that is upon Jesus to bind up and heal our (parents' and child's) broken hearts. Give us the ability to understand and forgive one another as God for Christ's sake has forgiven us. Thank You for the Holy Spirit Who leads us into all truth and corrects erroneous perceptions about past or present situations.

Thank You for teaching us to listen to each other and giving _____ an ear that hears admonition for then he/she will be called wise. I affirm that I will speak excellent and princely things and the opening of my lips shall be for right things. Father, I commit to train and teach _____ in the way that he/she is to go and when _____ is old he/she will not depart from sound doctrine and teaching, but will follow it all the days of his/her life. In the name of Jesus, I command rebellion to be far from the heart of my child and confess that he/she is willing and obedient, free to enjoy the reward of Your promises. _____ shall be peaceful bringing peace to others.

Father, according to Your Word we have been given the ministry of reconciliation and I release this ministry and the word of reconciliation into this family situation. I refuse to provoke or irritate or fret my child, I will not be hard on him/her lest he/she becomes discouraged, feeling inferior and frustrated. I will not break his/her spirit in the name of Jesus and by the power of the Holy

Spirit. Father, I forgive my child for the wrongs which he/she has done and stand in the gap until he/she comes to his/her senses and escapes out of the snare of the enemy (rebellion). Thank You for watching over Your Word to perform it, turning and reconciling the heart of the rebellious child to the parents and the hearts of the parents to the child. Thank You for bringing my child back into a healthy relationship with You and with me that our lives might glorify You! Amen.

Scripture References

Psalm 55:12-14	Proverbs 8:6,7
1 Peter 5:7	Proverbs 22:6
Psalm 37:4	Isaiah 1:19
John 14:6	Isaiah 54:13
Ephesians 6:1-3	2 Corinthians 5:18,19
1 John 1:9	Colossians 3:21
Isaiah 61:1	John 20:23
John 16:13	Ezekial 22:30
Proverbs 15:31	Jeremiah 1:12
Proverbs 13:1	Malachi 4:6

Comfort for a Person Who Has Lost a Christian Loved One

Father, I thank You that we have a High Priest Who is able to understand and sympathize and have a fellow feeling with_____'s weaknesses and infirmities (grief over the loss of his/her_____). Therefore, I fearlessly and confidently and boldly draw near to the throne of grace; that _____ may receive mercy and find grace to help in good time for every need — appropriate and well-timed help, coming just when _____ needs it.

Father, I thank You that _____ does not sorrow, as one who has no hope, because he/she believes that Jesus died and rose again; even so his/her loved one also who sleeps in Jesus will God bring back with Him. I ask that You comfort _____, for You said, **Blessed are they that mourn: for they shall be comforted** (Matt. 5:4).

Jesus, You have come to heal the brokenhearted. It is in the name of Jesus that You, Father, comfort _____ because You have loved him/her and have

PRAYERS THAT AVAIL MUCH COMMEMORATIVE GIFT EDITION

given him/her everlasting consolation and good hope through grace.

Blessed be God, even the Father of our Lord Jesus Christ, the Father of mercies, and the God of all comfort; Who comforts _____ in all his/her tribulation, that he/she may be able to comfort those which are in any trouble, by the comfort wherewith he himself/she herself is comforted by God.

Father, thank You for appointing unto _____ who mourns in Zion, to give unto him/her beauty for ashes, the oil of joy for mourning, the garment of praise for the spirit of heaviness; that he/she might be called a tree of righteousness, the planting of the Lord, that You might be glorified.

In Jesus' name, amen.

Scripture References

Hebrews 4:15,16 AMP   2 Thessalonians 2:16

1 Thessalonians 4:13b,14   2 Corinthians 1:3,4

Matthew 5:4   Isaiah 61:3

Luke 4:18

Healing of the Handicapped

Father, we come before you boldly and confidently knowing that You are not a man that You should lie and that You watch over Your Word to perform it. Therefore, Father, we bring before You those who are called handicapped and ill — mentally and physically. Father, by the authority of Your Word, we know without a doubt that it is Your will for these people — babies, children, and adults — to be made completely whole and restored in the name of Jesus.

We know, Father, that Satan, the god of this world, comes against Your handiwork. We know that You are the God of miracles, the God of love, power, and might. Through Your redemptive plan, what Jesus did on the cross and in the pit of hell for us, we, Your people, are redeemed from the curse of the law. The law of the Spirit of life in Christ Jesus has made us free from the law of sin and death. We are seated with Christ in heavenly places far above all satanic forces.

So we bring these people before Your throne of grace who have been attacked mercilessly mentally and physically — by Satan and his cohorts. We intercede in behalf of them and their families and loved ones.

Satan, we speak to you and to the principalities, powers, rulers of the darkness of this world, and wicked spirits in heavenly places, and we bind you and loose them from your assignments against these people in the mighty name of the Lord Jesus. You can no longer harass or hinder these people who have the opportunity this day to make Jesus their Lord and Savior. We bind doubt, unbelief, fear, tradition, discouragement, depression, and oppression from operating against the parents, children, and individuals involved.

Father, we pray for born-again, Spirit-filled people in positions of authority — administrators, teachers, doctors, nurses, orderlies, attendants, and volunteers. We pray that men and women of integrity, blameless and complete in Your sight, remain in these positions, but that the wicked be cut off and the treacherous be rooted out. Father, we pray for laborers of the harvest to go forth preaching the good news to the lost and to the Body of Christ.

We pray that You quicken these people to Your Word — that they be filled with wisdom and revelation knowledge concerning the integrity of Your Word, speaking faith-filled words and doing faith-filled actions. We pray for the infilling of the Holy Spirit, divine health, the fruit of the recreated human spirit, the gifts of the Holy Spirit, and deliverance. May they know that Jesus is their Source of every consolation, comfort, and encouragement and that they are to be sanctified spirit, soul, and body. We confess that they are redeemed from the curse of the law — redeemed from every sickness, disease, malady, affliction, defect, deficiency, deformity, injury, and every demon.

We speak healing to unborn infants in the wombs of mothers for **Lo, children are an heritage of the Lord and the fruit of the womb is his reward** (Ps. 127:3).

We speak restoration to damaged brain cells and activation of dormant brain cells. We speak normal intellect for one's age. We speak creative miracles to the parts of the body. We speak healing to all wounds. We speak words of life and say that they shall live in victory in this life and not die. We speak perfect soundness of mind and wholeness in body and spirit. We say that tongues are loosed and speech is distinct. We say ears hear and eyes see in the name of Jesus. We say demons are cast out bowing to the name of Jesus. We speak deliverance to bodies and minds, for You, Lord God, are the help of their countenance and the lifter of those bowed down — the joy of the Lord is their strength and stronghold!

We commission God's ministering spirits to go forth as they hearken to God's Word to provide the necessary help for and assistance to those we are praying for!

Father, no Word of Yours is void of the power that it takes to cause itself to come to pass! We establish Your Word on this earth, for it is already forever settled in heaven. Nothing is too hard or impossible for You. All things are possible to us who believe. We pray for more intercessors to stand with us. Let our prayers be set forth as incense before You — a sweet fragrance to You! Praise the Lord!

In Your name we pray, amen.

Scripture References

Romans 3:4	Mark 16:17
Mark 11:23,24	Jeremiah 1:12
Psalm 42:11	1 Peter 2:24
Acts 3:16	Psalm 146:8
Matthew 8:17	2 Corinthians 4:4
Nehemiah 8:10	Mark 7:35
John 10:10	Psalm 103:20
Proverbs 20:12	Galations 3:13
Matthew 9:37,38	Luke 1:37
Romans 8:2	Ephesians 1:17,18
Psalm 119:89	Ephesians 2:6
2 Corinthians 1:3	Jeremiah 32:27
Matthew 18:18	1 Thessalonians 5:23
Mark 9:23	Proverbs 2:21,22
Psalm 127:3	Psalm 141:2

Those Involved in Abortion
Introduction

Through our ministry, a dear child of God shared with us the following Scriptures which continue to bring her through periods of grief and sorrow. God's grace and love have proven to be the balm necessary for healing the emotional pain incurred by an act that cannot be reversed. The memory of the decision which was made will never be erased. Reminders are all around — at church, in the media, and in everyday life.

The prayer as written has a two-fold application: 1) for a people — a nation — who has permitted the legalization of abortion on demand; 2) for both the man and woman involved in the decision-making process. During moments of intercession for women and men who are dealing with past mistakes, we have identified with them in their pain. God's Word is the medicine that heals, and the salvation of souls.

Prayer [1]

Father, in the name of Jesus, forgive us as a nation for disregarding the sanctity of life. We recognize that

---

[1] This prayer can also be prayed in the singular "I" form by the individual person involved in abortion.

eachperson is uniquely created by You, Lord —
marvelously made! You know each one inside and out,
You know every bone in the body. You know exactly
how we are made, bit by bit, how we are sculpted from
nothing into something. All the stages of a life are
spread out before you, and the days are prepared before
a child even lives one day. Since we now see clearly, we
value the life You give.

Father, each of us is an open book to You; even
from a distance, You know what we are thinking. We
are never out of Your sight. When we look back, we
realize that You were there. You were present when we
put to death the being/beings to whom You gave life.

Lord, we repent of our sin, and the sin of our
nation. Be merciful unto us, O Lord. We ask Your
forgiveness, and You are faithful and just to forgive us
and cleanse us from all unrighteousness.

Unless Your law had been our delight, we would
have perished in our affliction. We will never forget
Your precepts, [how can we?] for it is by them You have
quickened us (granted us life).

We are ready to halt and fall; our pain and sorrow are continually before us. For we do confess our guilt and iniquity; we are filled with sorrow for our sin.

So [instead of further rebuke, now] we desire rather to turn and be [graciously] forgiven and comforted and encouraged to keep us from being overwhelmed by excessive sorrow and despair.

We look to Jesus as our Savior and consolation, and welcome His peace and completeness to our soul. We cannot bring our child/children back again; we shall go to them, they will not return to us.

We are awaiting and looking for the [fulfillment, the realization of our] blessed hope, even the glorious appearing of our great God and Savior Christ Jesus (the Messiah, the Anointed One).

In His name we pray, amen.

Scripture References

Psalm 139:14-16	Psalm 119:92,93 AMP
MESSAGE	2 Corinthians 2:7 AMP

Psalm 38:17,18 AMP   2 Samuel 12:23 AMP
Psalm 139:2-5 MESSAGE   Titus 2:13 AMP
1 John 1:9

An AIDS Patient

I.

Prayer for the Child of God

Father, You sent Jesus to bind up _____'s heartaches and to heal his/her emotional and physical pain. The Bible says that You sent Your Word to heal him/her and to deliver _____ from all his/her destructions.

Lord, we believe; help our unbelief. We ask You to give _____ a spirit of wisdom and revelation [of insight into mysteries and secrets] in the [deep and intimate] knowledge of Jesus, the Messiah.

Father, as _____ grows in grace and the knowledge of the Lord Jesus Christ, help him/her to receive all the spiritual blessings given by You. Thank You for giving him/her peace that the world cannot take away.

Lord, Your Son Jesus gave His life for _____. He/she has received Him as his/her Lord, and is born again, desiring to give the glory to You and to continue to fellowship with Your family. Jesus lives in his/her heart, and he/she loves You and loves others as he/she loves himself/herself. Thank You that _____ finds plenty of support from the Body of Christ so that he/she will find encouragement, edification, and comfort.

Heavenly Father, in Your mercy strengthen _____ and help him/her with his/her physical problems. Let him/her be aware that he/she is not alone, for there is nothing that can separate him/her from the love of Christ — not pain, or stress, or persecution. He/she will come to the top of every circumstance or trial through Jesus' love.

Father, _____ is trusting in You and doing good; so shall he/she dwell in the land and feed surely on Your faithfulness, and truly he/she shall be fed. _____ delights himself/herself also in You, and You will give him/her the desires and secret petitions of his/her heart. We ask You to give _____ the grace to commit his/her way to You, trusting in You, and You will bring it to pass.

Help _____ to enter into Your rest, Lord, and to wait for You without fretting himself/herself. May he/she cease from unrighteous anger and wrath.

Father, You have not given _____ a spirit of fear; but of power, and of love, and of a sound mind. Neither shall he/she be confounded and depressed. You have given him/her beauty for ashes, the oil of joy for mourning, and the garment of praise for the spirit of heaviness, that You might be glorified.

The chastisement [needful to obtain] _____'s peace and well-being was upon Jesus, and with the stripes [that wounded] Him, he/she was healed and made whole.

As Your child, Father, _____ has a joyful and confident hope of eternal salvation. This hope will never disappoint or delude him/her, for Your love has been poured out in his/her heart through the Holy Spirit Who has been given to him/her.

In the name of Jesus, amen.

Scripture References

Luke 4:18 AMP

Psalm 107:20

Mark 9:24

Ephesians 1:17 AMP

2 Peter 3:18

Ephesians 1:3

John 14:27

John 3:3

John 13:34

Romans 8:35-37

2 Corinthians 2:14

Psalm 37:3-5,7,8 AMP

2 Timothy 1:7

Isaiah 54:4 AMP

Isaiah 61:3

Isaiah 53:5 AMP

Romans 5:4,5 AMP

II.

Prayer for One Who Does Not Know Jesus as Lord

Thank You for calling us to be Your agents of intercession for _____. By the grace of God we will build
up the wall and stand in the gap before You for _____
that he/she might be spared from eternal destruction.

Lord, we acknowledge Your Son Jesus as the Lamb
of God Who takes away _____'s sins. Thank
You for sending the Holy Spirit Who goes forth to

convince and convict _____ of sin, righteousness, and judgment. Your kindness leads him/her to repent (to change his/her mind and inner man to accept Your will). You are the One Who delivers _____ and draws him/her to Yourself out of the control and dominion of darkness and transfers him/her into the Kingdom of the Son of Your love.

Lord of the harvest, we ask You to thrust the perfect laborer into _____'s path, a laborer to share Your Gospel in a special way so he/she will listen and understand it. We believe that he/she will come to his/her senses — come out of the snare of the devil who has held him/her captive — and make Jesus the Lord of his/her life.

Father, as _____ grows in grace and the knowledge of the Lord Jesus Christ, help him/her to receive all the spiritual blessings given by You. Thank You for giving him/her peace that the world cannot take away.

Heavenly Father, in Your mercy strengthen _____ and help him/her with his/her physical problems. Let him/her be aware that he/she is not alone, for there is nothing that can separate him/her from the love of Christ — not pain, or stress, or persecution. He/she will come to the top of every circumstance or trial through Jesus' love.

Help _____ to enter into Your rest and to wait for You without fretting himself/herself. May he/she cease from unrighteous anger and wrath.

Father, You sent Jesus to bind up _____'s heartaches and to heal his/her emotional and physical pain. The Bible says that You sent Your Word to heal him/her and to deliver _____ from all his/her destructions. We ask You to give him/her a spirit of wisdom and revelation [of insight into mysteries, and secrets] in the [deep and intimate] knowledge of Jesus, the Messiah.

The chastisement [needful to obtain] _____'s peace and well-being was upon Jesus, and with the stripes that wounded Him he/she was healed and made whole. As Your child, Father, _____ has a joyful and confident hope of eternal salvation. This hope will never disappoint or delude him/her, for Your love has been poured out in his/her heart through the Holy Spirit Who has been given to him/her.

In the name of Jesus, amen.

Scripture References

Ezekiel 22:30 AMP

John 1:29

John 16:8-12 AMP

Romans 2:4 AMP

Colossians 1:13 AMP

Matthew 9:38 AMP

2 Timothy 2:26 NIV

2 Peter 3:18

Ephesians 1:3

John 14:27

Romans 8:35-37

2 Corinthians 2:14

Psalm 37:7,8 AMP

Luke 4:18 AMP

Psalm 107:20

Ephesians 1:17 AMP

Isaiah 53:5 AMP

Romans 5:5

Prison Inmates

Introduction

The following prayers were written in response to
letters from prisoners requesting prayers to be used by
them in special circumstances. They may be prayed in
agreement with a prayer partner or intercessor.

I.

Prayer for an Inmate's Protection and Future

Father, I pray that I may become useful and helpful
and kind to those around me, tenderhearted (compassionate, understanding, loving-hearted), forgiving others
[readily and freely], as You, Father, in Christ forgave me
my sins.

It is my desire to be an imitator of You, Lord. With
the Holy Spirit as my Helper, I will [copy You and
follow Your example], as a well-beloved child [imitates
his/her father]. I purpose to walk in love, [esteeming
and delighting in others] as Christ loves me. As I attend

to Your Word, I depend on Your Holy Spirit to teach me to live a life of victory in Christ Jesus my Lord.

In the name of Jesus, I am Your child. I am dwelling in the secret place of the Most High and abiding under the shadow of the Almighty. I say of You, Lord, that You are my Refuge and Fortress: my God; in You will I trust. You cover me with Your feathers, and under Your wings shall I trust: Your truth is my shield and buckler.

Because You are my Lord, my Refuge and Habitation, no evil shall befall me — no accident will overtake me — neither shall any plague or calamity come near me. You give Your angels [especial] charge over me, to keep me in all of my ways [of obedience and service].

Thank You for hearing my prayer. You are with me in trouble; You deliver me, and satisfy me with long life and show me Your salvation.

In Jesus' name, amen.

Scripture References

Ephesians 4:32 AMP	Psalm 91:9-11 AMP
Ephesians 5:1,2 AMP	Psalm 91:15,16
Psalm 91:1,2,4	

II.

Prayer for an Incarcerated Parent and His/Her Children

Listen, God, I'm calling at the top of my lungs: "Be good to me! Answer me!"

When my heart whispered, "Seek God," my whole being replied, "I'm seeking Him!" Don't hide from me now.

I didn't know it before, but I know now that You've always been right here for me; don't turn Your back on me now. Don't throw me out, don't abandon me; You've always kept the door open.

Thank You for sending ministers to tell me about You and Your love for me.

My children say they hate me, they feel abandoned and alone. Even though their father/mother walked away from them, I ask You, Father, to take them in.

Lord of the harvest, I ask You to send laborers of the harvest and wise counselors to my children who have been hurt by my actions.

Father, I have sinned against You, against my children, and against myself. I repent of the sins that have so easily beset me, and ask You to forgive me.

Father, Your Word assures me that You forgive me and cleanse me from all unrighteousness. Thank You for forgiving me. I pray that my children will be willing to forgive me so that we may be a family again.

In the name of Jesus, I cast the care of my children on You and rest in the assurance that You will perfect that which concerns me. I put on the garment of praise, and delight myself in You. Teach me Your ways, O Lord, that I may walk and live in Your truth.

In Jesus' name, amen.

Scripture References

Psalm 27:7-10 MESSAGE	Psalm 138:8
Matthew 9:38	Isaiah 61:3
1 John 1:9	Psalm 37:4
1 Peter 5:7	Psalm 86:11 AMP

III.

Prayer for an Inmate to Pray for His/Her Family and Caregiver

Father, I have sinned against You, against my children, and against myself. I repent of the sins that have so easily beset me, asking Your forgiveness.

Father, Your Word assures me that You forgive me and cleanse me from all unrighteousness. Thank You for forgiving me. I pray that my children will be willing to forgive me so that we may be a family again.

Thank You for the one who has assumed responsibility for my children while I am away. I pray that You will strengthen him/her and fill him/her with Your Spirit Who gives him/her great wisdom, ability, and skill in rearing the children You gave to me. I repent for failing to assume my responsibility to my children, and ask You to reward the one who is taking care of them.

His/her mouth shall speak of wisdom; and the meditation of his/her heart shall be understanding. I thank You that he/she is in Christ Jesus, Who has been made unto him/her wisdom from You — his/her righteousness, holiness, and redemption. He/she is filled with the knowledge of Your will in all spiritual wisdom and understanding so that he/she may live a life worthy of You and may please You in every way, bearing fruit in every good work.

Father, I am responsible for my own actions, and I recognize that what I have done has hurt my entire family. Forgive me for dishonoring You, my family, my friends, and my children. Give me the grace to pay my debt, and do my assigned work as unto You. Help me to develop diligence and patience, giving myself to prayer, study, and meditation in Your Word.

Lord, there is violence within these walls, but I look to You. Hide me in the secret place of Your presence from the plots of others. Keep me secretly in Your pavilion from the strife of tongues.

In the name of Jesus I pray, amen.

Scripture References

1 John 1:9	Colossians 1:9,10 AMP
Psalm 49:3	Colossians 3:23,24
1 Corinthians 1:30	Psalm 31:20

About the Author

Germaine Griffin Copeland, founder and president of Word Ministries, Inc., is the author of the *Prayers That Avail Much Family Books*. Her writings provide scriptural prayer instruction to help you pray effectively for those things that concern you and your family and for other prayer assignments. Her teachings on prayer, the personal growth of the intercessor, emotional healing and related subjects have brought understanding, hope, healing and liberty to the discouraged and emotionally wounded. She is a woman of prayer and praise whose highest form of worship is the study of God's Word. Her greatest desire is to know God.

Word Ministries, Inc. is a prayer and teaching ministry. Germaine believes that God has called her to teach the practical application of the Word of Truth for successful, victorious living. After years of searching diligently for truth, and trying again and again to come out of depression, she decided that she was a mistake. Out of the depths of despair she called upon the name of the Lord, and the Light of God's presence invaded the room where she was sitting.

It was in that moment that she experienced the warmth of God's love; old things passed away and she felt brand new. She discovered a motivation for living — life had purpose. Living in the presence of God she has found unconditional love and acceptance, healing for crippled emotions, contentment that overcomes depression, peace in the midst of adverse circumstances, and grace for developing healthy relationships. The ongoing process of transformation evolved into praying for others, and the prayer of intercession became her prayer focus.

Germaine is the daughter of Reverend A. H. "Buck" Griffin and the late Donnis Brock Griffin. She and her husband, Everette, have four children, five grandchildren and two great-grandchildren. Germaine and Everette reside in Sandy Springs, a suburb of Atlanta, Georgia.

Word Ministries' offices are located in Historic Roswell, 38 Sloan Street, Roswell, Georgia 30075. Telephone: 770-518-1065

You may contact
Word Ministries
by writing

Word Ministries, Inc.
38 Sloan Street
Roswell, Georgia 30075
or calling 770-518-1065
www.prayers.org

*Please include
your prayer requests
and comments when you write.*

MISSION STATMENT
Word Ministries, Inc.
To motivate individuals to spiritual growth and
emotional wholeness, encouraging them to become
more deeply and inimately acquainted with the
Father God as they pray prayers that avail much.

The Harrison House Vision

Proclaiming the truth and the power

Of the Gospel of Jesus Christ

With excellence;

Challenging Christians to

Live victoriously,

Grow spiritually,

Know God intimately.